SHADOW ONE

Derrick M. Jackson

Published by Ebony Blade Productions Fredericksburg, VA
Contact: Ebonybladeproductions@gmail.com

Editor: Tia Ross, tiarosseditor.com
Proof Reader: Vickie Harris

For Kaden, Keion, and Kameron.
Inspired by an Angel.

ACKNOWLEDGMENTS

First, I want to thank my Father in Heaven, whose divine authority has guided me my entire life. I thank him for his grace and for allowing me to experience the things I've done, to see the things I've seen and to have a mind to express myself through written word to share those experiences.

Next, I would like to thank my family. They have supported me from Day One, and always provided the foundation for me to stand. I hope this book inspires you as much as you have inspired me through the years.

I want to give my thanks to two exceptional people who were very influential in the creation of this novel. Air Force Special Agent (Retired) Wayne Sparks and Special Agent (Retired) Vic Zuege. Your mentorship and friendship was instrumental in my development as an Agent and provided the backbone for SHADOW ONE. In addition, to everyone who has held the title of Special Agent with the Air Force Office of Special Investigations, you have my utmost respect for what you've done and continue to do for this nation.

Thank you very much to a few special people who encouraged me throughout this process, provided invaluable counsel, and the motivation that I needed to keep going!

DJ

TABLE OF CONTENTS

SHADOW ONE

Based on a True Story

CHAPTER 1
I THOUGHT I WAS YOUR DREAM

Aiea, Hawaii – 1845 hours

A garage door opened at a townhouse perched in the mountains overlooking Pearl Harbor. Inside, Air Force Staff Sergeant Devin Jackson, a sometimes-quiet southern man from Alabama, was preparing to start his day. Despite being on active duty, his five o'clock shadow was his way of rebelling against the military's grooming standards. Devin's focus on their future often put him at odds with his girlfriend, Tori, who preferred living in the moment.

As Devin started his motorcycle, his phone vibrated with a text from Tori: "You on your way?"

He pulled out of the neighborhood and onto the H-1 Highway, where the scenery was breathtaking—battleships and aircraft carriers were moored in the bay to his right. He was on his way to Tori's apartment in Honolulu, overlooking Waikiki Beach.

Upon arrival, he took the elevator to the sixth floor and knocked twice. The door swung open to reveal Tori, a twenty-seven-year-old with a strong mind and a mane of long, bushy hair. She eyed Devin like a lioness growing tired of her cub's antics. Tori, also in the Air Force, had been a medical assistant for seven years.

"You must've gotten lost again on the one highway from my house to yours," Tori said.

"My bad, T. Are you ready?" Devin asked.

"Yeah, let me grab my purse. Wait … what are you driving?"

Devin smiled and showed the key in his hand. "You already know."

Tori loved motorcycles. She didn't own one but had grown up riding on her brother's back in Georgia and relished any chance to ride Devin's. After a celebratory dance, Tori ran back into her bedroom and grabbed her helmet, then took the key from Devin's hand. "Hey, babe, lock the door for me," she said, running out of the apartment. By the time Devin reached his bike, Tori was already seated with her helmet on, ready to ride. She lifted her visor. "Hop on the back!"

Devin frowned, not amused by her intention of driving. "If you don't get your hips to the back!"

Tori puffed out her lips, closed her visor, and slid to the back of the motorcycle.

They headed out, driving past Diamond Head and winding along roads flanked by the Jurassic mountains on their left and the violent shoreline on their right. They arrived at the Hawaiian Cultural Center and spent the next two hours enjoying local cuisine and dancing. Later, they parked alongside the giant rocks on the Leeward side of the island, where the ocean's mist sprayed high into the air and waves smashing into the large boulders. Sitting on the rocks, Devin and Tori enjoyed the height of their romance, listening to music and watching the waves.

"Are you staying at my place tonight?" Tori asked as mist gently landed on their shoulders.

Devin looked away. "Nah, I've got roll call tomorrow at O-6."

"That's cool," Tori said. "You can stay at my place and leave for work in the morning."

Devin laughed. "I can't, T. I don't have my uniform with me."

Tori frowned at being turned down for the night. "Ugh, well, how about you come up for just a little while?"

Devin kissed her cheek. "Now you know there's no such thing as 'just a little while' with us. Come on, it's getting late, and we need to get going. But I owe you."

"Yes, you do," Tori mumbled.

The next morning, at 0530, Devin arrived at Hickam Air Force Base, showed his ID to the Security Forces guard, and was waved onto the base. As a ten-year veteran assigned to the 735th Air Mobility Squadron as a jet engine specialist, Devin spent twelve to fourteen hours a day working on various transport aircraft. Hickam AFB, with its manicured landscapes, tall palm trees, and vibrant tropical flowers, looked more like a resort than a fully functioning military installation.

Devin parked beside Hanger 9, an aircraft hangar bearing scars of the December 7 attack—one wall still had bullet holes as proof. He was a few minutes early, so he went to the break room to check the daily assignment list and saw that he, Mike, and a new guy, Senior Airman Brown, were assigned to a B model C-5 Galaxy aircraft, 70-0213. Relieved to find he would be conducting an engine run to evaluate a newly installed fuel flow transmitter, Devin felt eager. Although being an Air Force jet mechanic was tough, operating the jet engines was a job he would have done every day for free. It was the reason he joined the Air Force in the first place.

At the flight line, Devin and Mike parked at the wingtip of the massive C-5. They agreed Devin would "sit sticks" (operate the jet engines from the pilot's seat) while Mike managed the flight engineer's panel. Mike was a C-5 crew chief who had been working on the aircraft for twelve years. He headed upstairs to the cockpit to review the aircraft forms and began his engine-start checklist. Meanwhile, Devin was being pushed around on a B-5 stand by Airman Brown. The TF-39 engines on the C-5 were large enough for Devin to climb inside the inlet, stretch his hands above his head, and still not reach the top. He conducted the inspection by slowly spinning and examining each fan blade, ensuring there were no loose rivets or debris inside the inlet. He then jumped back onto the stand, and Brown pushed him around the sides of the engines to examine the thrust reversers and finally the engine exhaust.

Devin turned his attention to the landing gear and the exterior of the C-5. The sound of the auxiliary power units spooling up told Devin exactly where Mike was in his checklist. After about an hour, the outside inspection was completed. Devin did a quick walk through in the cargo bay and headed upstairs to the cockpit to join Mike and Airman Brown. Mike had finished his checklist and appeared to be fiddling around with the gauges by swapping the fuel between the main tanks.

Devin opened the crew door at the top of the stairs and joined Mike and Airman Brown in the cockpit. The condensation from the air conditioner was so thick he could barely see his hand in front of his face. What was visible was a medley of flashing lights shining through from the engineer's panel. Devin climbed into the pilot's seat and checked the radio settings.

"Y'all boys ready?" Devin asked, plugging in his headset.

"Yeah, man, waiting on you," Mike replied, turning off the air conditioning. Airman Brown was sitting in the co-pilot's seat, looking extremely nervous.

"Hey Devin, man, I've never done this before," Brown said.

Devin, sensing Brown's uncertainty, decided against playing a prank. The problem was, Mike was much better at playing pranks and sometimes did not know when to end it. Devin decided to play it straight and gave Brown a quick tutorial on his responsibilities. "Hey man, it's no big deal. Basically, you have two jobs: call the tower once the engines start and flip the brake switch to 'emergency' if the brakes fail," said Devin.

Brown nodded as though he understood his instructions, but Devin was prepared to remind him again in the unlikely event that an emergency occurred. With everything set, they were ready to run the engines.

Mr. Terry, a local Hawaiian who held a civilian job as an aircraft mechanic in the squadron, arrived at the aircraft and plugged his headset into the cord while standing in front of it. Devin called down to him to ensure there were no hazards in front or behind the aircraft before starting the engine. Once Mr. Terry gave the all-clear, Devin and Mike began the engine start sequence.

Devin: "Here we go. Button in on one."

Mike: "Pressure drop."

Mr. Terry: "Rotation."

Mike: "Fuel flow … positive oil."

Devin: "N1."

Mike: "TIT"

Devin: "LOP light out. Good idle. Mr. Terry, is the TR clear?"

Terry: "Yes, number one TR is clear."

Devin grabbed the throttle for the number one engine, lifted it up and over the gate, and slowly brought it backward to open the thrust reverser.

Mike: "Good pressure."

Terry: "TR open … and closed."

Devin and the crew continued the checklist until all four engines had been started. Once all the engines were idle, Devin set the timer for five minutes. This allowed the engines to stabilize, and it also gave Mike a few more minutes to complete his checklist to ensure that all systems were operating. Mr. Terry extended the headphone cord to its full fifty-foot length in front of the aircraft. Mike indicated the checklist was completed, and he was ready to proceed with the run.

Devin grabbed all four throttles with his right hand and slowly pushed them forward. The engines on the C-5 did not respond instantly like those on fighter jets, so Devin needed to be careful not to let the engine speed and temperature get ahead of him, which could cause the engine to over-temp or over-speed. As the jet engines spooled up, the thrust increased, causing the aircraft to shake violently. Devin glanced quickly at Airman Brown, who looked both amazed and frightened at the same time.

"Alright, Mike, that's 90 percent. How's your fuel flow?" Devin asked.

"Fuel flow is in the green. Looking good!"

"Roger, I'm reading the same from up here. I'm going to take two and three up to take-off power," Devin said.

Airman Brown had no idea what the two mechanics were talking about, but something about the phrase "take-off power" made him even more anxious.

Sensing Brown's uneasiness, Devin gave a quick reminder. "Hey man, just remember, if the brakes fail and we jump chocks, flip the hydraulic brake switch to emergency. Got it?"

"Yeah, I got it, but what happens if the brakes fail?"

"As long you flip the switch, nothing much. We might move forward a few feet, but if you don't, we'll be taking Fat Freddie for a ride," Devin replied jokingly.

Mike heard the explanation and laughed loudly through the headset. Despite the jovial demeanor, Airman Brown remained anxious.

Devin took hold of the number two and three throttles and slowly pushed them forward toward the predetermined temperature and speed. Everyone on the base could hear the engines screaming. Mike watched the gauges closely from the flight engineer's panel. Once they reached the desired speed and temperature, Devin held the throttles in place.

"Alright, Mike, I'm reading TRT, and fuel flow is green. What do you see?" Devin asked.

"Yeah, looks good to me. Let it sit here for a couple of minutes just to make sure and if the fuel flow doesn't drop off, we can shut it down," Mike responded.

"Okay, you got it. We'll give it five minutes," Devin said.

It had taken many years of experience and several months of specific training to qualify for this task. Despite the litany of things that could go wrong at this moment, Devin felt at ease. He knew he could rely on his training and that Mike was just as comfortable with the situation as he was.

As Devin sat with his right hand still on the throttles, he glanced at the clock to time the engine shutdown. Suddenly, Mike interrupted with an unwelcome remark.

"Hey, do you guys smell that?"

Devin lifted his eyes from the engine gauges and slowly turned back toward Mike. At first, he thought Mike was joking and had relieved himself of gas as part of yet another prank. But then Devin caught a whiff of the scent and knew immediately it had not come from Mike.

"Yeah, I smell it too," Devin said.

The two mechanics quickly searched their individual gauges for any sign of a problem with the aircraft. Mike scanned the engineer's panel for any discrepancies, then he found one.

"Hey, I lost hydraulics on two and three…no, all four hydraulics are gone!" Mike yelled as he toggled the switches on his panel.

Out of disbelief, Devin initially turned back to the engineer's panel to double-check what Mike had told him. Then, remembering his training, he quickly retarded the throttles back to idle. "Brown, go down to the cargo bay and see what's going on!" Devin shouted.

Airman Brown, looking unsure of what was expected of him, unbuckled his seat belt, slid his chair back, and headed toward the crew entrance. As soon as Brown opened the crew door, a thick pink mist flowed in and filled the cockpit. Immediately, Devin and Mike recognized they had a severe hydraulic leak.

Devin instructed Mike to conduct an emergency shutdown of all engines, as the vapor from the hydraulic fluid was extremely flammable and one spark could cause an uncontrollable fire on an aircraft holding 200,000 pounds of fuel in just a matter of seconds. Devin called the Maintenance Operations Center over the aircraft radio to report the situation. "MOC, Maintenance

2, Maintenance 3, this is 213 with a ground emergency. We have a severe hydraulic leak in the cargo bay. Send a fire truck immediately!"

Brown stood in the doorway, fully engulfed by the mist, and screamed, "There's smoke in the cargo bay!"

Mike, busy with the emergency shutdown procedures, turned around to bark orders at the inexperienced Brown. "Grab a fire extinguisher, dumbass!"

Devin pulled the engine T-handles to shut off the fuel flow to the engines. Mike shut down both auxiliary power units, and the aircraft began to lose power as the engine generators slowly wound down. The cockpit lights were flickering on and off, and suddenly, the obnoxiously loud fire warning horn blared, sounding like a freight train driving through the cockpit. As the generators died, the engine gauges violently shot up and down as the power fluctuated for several seconds.

Finally, the power completely shut off, and Mike and Devin hustled down the stairs to the cargo bay. They saw no signs of a fire and noticed that Airman Brown had already made his way off the aircraft, so they followed him outside. Once they exited the aircraft, they found a host of vehicles had arrived. Several levels of management were standing at the bottom of the ladder, waiting for an explanation. The flight line production supervisor arrived in his blue pickup truck and made a beeline over to the maintenance crew.

"Which one of you is responsible for this aircraft?" he demanded.

Devin replied, "That's me. I was sitting sticks."

The flight line supervisor frowned and instructed Devin to report back to the Quality Assurance office to fill out a ground mishap report.

Embarrassed by all the attention, Devin made his way back to Hangar 9 and began to fill out the accident report. Even though the hydraulic leak was not due to his negligence, he knew convincing everyone else of that would be an uphill battle. Devin completed the report and handed it over to the Q.A. supervisor.

"Hey, the First Shirt called here looking for you. He wants you to report to his office as soon as you finish the paperwork," said the supervisor.

Devin, now believing that some rumor about what happened on the flight line had reached the First Sergeant, simply nodded, grabbed his keys from his locker, and headed out of the hangar. As he walked toward his vehicle, he received a text message from Tori: "Hey, dinner tonight?"

"Yes, it's been a rough day," he responded.

Tori texted back: "Okay, cool. Don't forget you still owe me."

Devin arrived at the Commander Support Staff Office and walked in to find the Shirt standing at the front desk waiting for him. "Sergeant, I heard you had an interesting morning," the First Sergeant said.

Devin felt a need to get ahead of the narrative. "Yes, I did. Honestly, it all happened fast. But I'm confident we handled it correctly and followed the emergency procedures."

To Devin's astonishment, the Shirt could not have cared less about what happened on the aircraft. "Well, regardless of what caused today's incident, it seems like you may have bigger issues to deal with."

Devin stood there confused, wondering what else he had done that could have gotten him into trouble.

The Shirt sensed Devin was unaware of the real reason he was summoned and threw him a clue. "Have you heard anything about your retraining application?"

"OSI? Did I get in?"

"I don't know all the details, but an agent called here a couple of hours ago. He said he was from the Office of Special Investigations and that you need to report to his office at ten hundred hours tomorrow morning. Are you sure this is what you want, son? Your life will never be the same."

"What do you mean by that?" Devin asked.

"Your friends will stop trusting you. People will always suspect you, and those closest to you will question your commitment to them. Make sure this is what you want to do before you agree to anything. Don't just think about what you're gaining. Think what you'll be losing too."

Later that night, Devin and Tori were walking together along Waikiki Beach at sunset. Over time, as the two became remarkably close, they realized they had a shared interest in music and history and enjoyed learning new things about each other. After a few months, the two became inseparable. Not only was

Tori his girlfriend, but she was also his best friend. As the two walked along the beach holding hands, Tori lay her head on his shoulder. Sensing that something was bothering him, she said, "So, you've been quiet tonight. What's going on? Is something wrong?"

Devin sighed. "Yeah, I've been trying to find the best time to tell you. I think I've got an assignment."

"I knew it!" Tori responded with excitement. "Are you coming with me to San Antonio?"

Devin turned his eyes away from her, dreading the heaviness of his response. "No, I'm going to FLETC."

"What the hell is FLETC?"

"The Federal Law Enforcement Training Center. Do you remember a few months ago I told you I applied for a position with OSI?" Devin wasn't really hoping for a response.

Tori released Devin's hands and took a few steps away from him. "OSI? Why would you want to do that? I thought you were coming to Texas with me."

"T, I told you I applied to OSI six months ago."

"Yeah, but I didn't think you'd really get accepted!"

Tori instantly regretted her words as soon as they came out of her mouth. They hit Devin like a gut punch, intensifying the doubts already swirling in his head about whether he could make it as an agent. He turned away from her, trying to hide how much her words had hurt him.

"Look, nothing has to change between us. I'm still me, and you're still you. Nothing changes," he said, his voice strained.

"What do you mean, nothing has to change?" Tori screamed.

Her voice was loud enough that other beachgoers turned to see what the commotion was about. Devin tried to calm her down by motioning with his hands for her to speak more quietly.

"No, don't tell me to calm down," Tori snapped. "You know my family's history with the police. Or did you somehow forget, Devin? They put my brother in a coma for two months. For what, looking suspicious? Looking like every other Black man that walks down the street? Then they lied and said it was his fault, and they coincidentally forgot to turn on their body cameras. And you knew this! So, tell me why would you want to do something like that? Why would you want to be one of them?"

Devin gave a huge sigh and laughed. Tori was quick to reprimand him. "I don't see anything to smile about. What's funny?"

Devin, feeling fed up with Tori's disrespect, responded, "This whole conversation sounds familiar. Ten years ago, before I joined the Air Force, the people I trusted the most asked me the same question. One by one, these men, who probably had my best interests in mind, all pulled me aside and asked, 'Why are you going into the Air Force? You should join the Army. A Black man ain't got no place in the Air Force.' Yet, here I am because it was the best choice for me. You know what? The first time I watched Top Gun, I fell in love with jets, so I became a jet mechanic. And now, my dream is to be a federal agent. Is that so bad?"

"That's a silly dream," Tori said.

"It may be a silly dream, but it's my dream," Devin replied, turning to stare out at the ocean.

Tori paused, a tear rolling down the left side of her face. "I thought I was your dream."

Without taking her eyes off Devin, Tori unchained her necklace. Devin stood motionless as his feet sank into the sand. No one said a word; the sound of the waves crashing on the beach seemed to symbolize their relationship ending abruptly. Tori grabbed Devin's right hand, placed the necklace inside it, and walked away.

"Tori, Tori, hold up, Tori!" Devin yelled. Before he could process what had transpired, he found himself standing alone and brokenhearted on the beach.

Tori quickly exited the beach and walked up the closest stairway to the street. Her heart pounded so hard she had to stop halfway up to catch her breath. She walked aimlessly on the sidewalk, not caring where her pain led her. Realizing people were staring at her and that she had no way home, she hurried down the street to flag down a taxi. She reached the car just as the driver was turning off his light for the night. Though he was inclined to turn her away, he felt sympathy for the beautiful young lady who was clearly in distress. Tori hopped in the back of the taxi, and the car pulled away. As they departed the beach area, they drove past Devin's motorcycle parked alongside the beach. Her heart sank even more as she stared at their matching helmets still connected to each other.

By this time, Devin was sitting at the edge of the water, his entire body numb. He paid little regard to his clothes getting wet as the rising tide submerged him chest-deep in the ocean. When he could no longer sit there, he stood and gazed out into the shadowy ocean. His mind was racing. He didn't know if he should be mad or heartbroken, but he was not ready to let her go—not that easily. Determined to make her see that this move could benefit both of them if they stayed together, he ran across the beach, up the stairway, and settled onto his bike.

Minutes later, Devin arrived at Tori's apartment building. He left his helmet on the bike and made his way to the front entrance, still dripping wet. As he approached the door, he felt someone's eyes on him. He turned to his right and saw Tori sitting on a bench in the park in front of her building. He stood there for a moment, realizing he had no idea what to say but knowing he wanted her beside him. He started walking toward her, and she stood up from the bench and ran to meet him. She ran into his arms, and after a quick embrace, began punching him in the chest.

Devin tried to stop her, but Tori, overcome with emotion, only punched harder. People in the park started noticing. Devin struggled to restrain her as she cried uncontrollably, asking, "Why would you do that? Why would you do that?" Some of her punches landed on Devin's face. Two women watching assumed Tori was being assaulted and ran to pull Devin away. Devin tried to push the women away to see about Tori, but they stood between him and her.

Moments later, the Honolulu police arrived and saw Devin pushing his way past the two women to get to Tori. Assuming they were witnessing an assault, they hurried over to restrain him. A young female officer pulled her weapon on Devin and began nervously screaming commands. Tori realized the situation had gotten out of control and started screaming at the female cop, who became even more unnerved.

"No Stop!" Tori screamed as a male officer tackled Devin into the side of his patrol car. Tori continued to proclaim Devin's innocence. "He didn't do anything! Put your guns down!" She was clearly triggered by the cops' response and finally locked eyes with Devin. "See, is this what you want for us? Is this what you want?"

After the commotion settled, Devin was released from detainment and instructed to leave the area. He didn't say a word as he made his way back to his bike, taking one last look at Tori, who was being held back by the police officers from saying goodbye. He started his motorcycle and drove away, watching as Tori's helmet fell to the ground and skidded against the curb.

Devin did not immediately return to his apartment. Instead, he drove to a jetty on the north side of Hickam's runway, a place where he and Tori had spent many hours laughing and contemplating their future together. This time, he was alone, standing there watching the waves crash against the rocks. A familiar sound caught his attention as two F-15s from Hickam taxied in front of him on their way to the runway. The pilots engaged the afterburners, and the two jets screamed into the night sky, their exhaust resembling comets' tails shooting across the heavens.

Devin's heart pulled him back to Tori, urging him to abandon his opportunity with the OSI. As he watched the jets surge into the night, a sense of calm washed over him. He realized that if he had not challenged himself to join the Air Force years ago, he would never have had the opportunity to stand where he was at that moment. Still torn by his pending decision, he stood at the water's edge, staring into the night, hoping to find an answer.

For reasons he couldn't understand, Devin walked into the darkness. He went further and further into the abyss until the weight of the waves crashing into his chest seemed to match the pain he was feeling. He continued walking, trudging deeper into the Pacific until the waves crested over his head. Pushing further, it took all his strength to fight for air, yet he kept going. The current took control, but he felt no fear. Unable to fight his way back to the surface, he sank under the waves, feeling a sense of calm as he watched the moonlight flicker in the clear water above him. He made no effort to resurface.

As he accepted what was happening, he heard a voice inside him: "Get up." Suddenly, the current violently swirled him back to the surface. Within minutes, it had pushed him close enough to the shore that he could walk back to the beach. A few people on the beach saw what had happened and watched intently as he dragged himself out of the water. Completely exhausted, he made his way across the sand and up to the street. Once he arrived at his bike, he sat on it long enough to regain his strength to safely drive home.

The next morning found Devin, dressed in his only suit, sitting in the parking lot outside the OSI Detachment on Hickam. It was 0930, and he still had not made his decision. He thumbed through pictures of Tori on his cell phone, wishing a stranger would tap on his window and tell him to go back to her.

At the same time, Tori was driving toward Pearl City, a few miles west of Hickam. She felt terrible for how she had treated Devin the night before and was even more regretful that he might think she had turned her back on him. Determined to set the record straight, she made a quick U-turn on the highway and headed back to Hickam, hoping to reach Devin before he agreed to join the OSI. She wanted him to know that she loved him and was willing to find a way to make it work.

It was 0945. Devin stepped out of his car and began walking to the front entrance of the detachment. Meanwhile, Tori was closing in on the airbase, just a couple of cars back from the entrance. She was shaking with nervousness, unsure of what she would say to Devin. Should she apologize and beg him to stay or simply support him as much as she could from a distance?

As Tori drove up to the security gate, she was met with horrible news from the Security Forces guard.

"Good afternoon, ma'am. I need you to pull to the side, please. Your car has been selected for a random vehicle search."

"What! No! I can't! I have to be somewhere!" Tori exclaimed, her voice tinged with desperation.

"Ma'am, I'm sorry, but your car is the twenty-fifth car, and we need to search it. Please pull to the side now."

Tori reluctantly pulled over and stepped out as the K-9 was brought out to search her car.

Devin began making his way up to the detachment's front door. With every step, he remembered the naysayers telling him not to follow his dreams. "That's not for Black people. You'll never get promoted. Your friends will turn their back on you." He recalled Tori's words from the night before: "I didn't think you'd really get accepted." The doubts weighed heavily on him, so much so that by the time he reached the door, he could barely lift his arm to reach the handle.

Tori was beside the guard shack having a meltdown when she realized she couldn't even call Devin because she had left her cell phone in the car. She tried to reach through the window to grab her phone from the cup holder, but the K-9 lunged at her, causing the Security Forces airmen to draw their weapons on her and force her to get face down on the concrete.

"You don't understand. I need my phone now. I need my phone!"

"Ma'am, I told you, when we're done, you're free to go, but not until then," one of the airmen responded firmly.

Devin's doubts seemed to have won. He turned away from the door and headed back to his car. After taking about ten steps, he started to regret his decision. He knew that if he stayed, he might eventually patch things up with Tori, but how long would it last if he was giving up his future for her? How long before animosity toward Tori wrecked their relationship, leaving him with nothing but "what if I had followed my dreams"? He paused, closed his eyes, and called out to the only person who could help him. "Yeshua, I don't know what to do. You've guided my entire life. Please don't leave me now. Help me go in the direction you want me to travel." Devin opens his eyes, confident in his decision but sad about his loss, then turned, walked up to the door, and stepped inside.

Security Forces finished their inspection, and Tori hurried back to her car. Her clothes were covered in dirt from being laid out on the side of the road. She picked up her cell phone and called Devin. His phone began to vibrate, showing that Tori was calling. No one answered. The phone was left inside his car.

CHAPTER 2
THE STRUGGLE IS REAL

Two weeks later

Devin began training at the OSI Academy to become an agent. The first obstacle was the Criminal Investigator Training Program at FLETC. The OSI training marked a significant change from his previous decade in the Air Force. The military uniform was gone, and he walked into the first day of training wearing a suit and tie. As expected, everyone in the class had a worried look on their face. The room was filled with about forty-five hopeful candidates, all aware that some of them would go home empty-handed.

As the students sat quietly before the instructor arrived, Devin noticed that all the Black students were giving each other "the nod." They had expected to be among maybe three or four Black students, but they were all shocked to find that about 25 percent of the class comprised Black airmen—Tuskegee would have been proud. To everyone's credit, they all worked together, showing respect for each other's journey without any unnecessary competitiveness.

The first cadre member to arrive was an instructor from the OSI Special Investigations Academy, located inside one of the buildings on the FLETC campus. He introduced himself and reminded the class that although they were going through training with the Department of Homeland Security, they would still be held to Air Force standards. After a few minutes of basic greetings, he wished the class well and said he would see them in two months. For those fortunate students who made it through the two-month long Criminal Investigations Training Program, they would immediately start another two months of training with the OSI Academy.

Finally, the class was greeted by a FLETC instructor who handed out the training curriculum. The room was filled with gasps of disbelief as the instructor meticulously went through the training schedule for the next two months. As Devin reviewed the curriculum, he could not help but feel excited for the days dedicated to emergency response driving, arrest techniques, and interrogations. However, he was less enthusiastic about the days filled with classroom lectures on constitutional amendments and infant death investigations.

It didn't take long for the class to get into the training rhythm. Physical training was part of the curriculum two or three times a week, mostly consisting of calisthenics, followed by a three- or four-mile run in the Georgia heat. However, that wasn't the only physical activity the trainees endured; they also had multiple classes a week in defensive tactics and arrest techniques. Most of the trainees seemed to enjoy the physical training until it was time to be evaluated. Everyone was excited to learn how to apply handcuffs, but the fun disappeared when they were assessed and only had a few seconds to get it done correctly.

As the training continued, everything introduced to the trainees at the beginning had to be evaluated by the end of the course for them to graduate. Midway through the course, the instructors taught how to properly search a suspect for weapons and contraband. The class got a good laugh during the exercises as they took turns hiding small objects on their persons while their teammates struggled to locate them. Everyone felt certain that the final exam for searches would be a breeze until they arrived for the tests and learned that they wouldn't be searching each other. Instead, the instructors had hired role players from the community to be searched.

The trainees waited in the hallway for their name to be called, then entered the room to give verbal commands to their role player. Once the role player was under control, the trainees conducted a thorough and sometimes invasive search. Each role player had at least one item on them, and if the trainee did not find it, they would fail the exam and possibly be removed from training, as was the norm with all the other training scenarios.

Devin's name was called, and he walked into the room to see which role player he had been assigned. To his surprise, standing in front of him was an attractive twenty-something white female wearing only spandex pants and a bra. He began to worry, as he didn't immediately see many places where the female could have hidden any contraband.

Devin started by giving her verbal commands and then began to search her body, starting with her hair. Finding nothing, he moved to the back of her bra strap. Feeling awkward and afraid of a potential sexual harassment complaint, he quickly checked under the strap and moved down to search the female's pants.

The lady's pants were skintight, so he used the back of his hands to ensure there were no hidden objects. Devin instructed the role player to remove her shoes, hoping to find an object hidden somewhere in her sneakers, but found nothing. Time was running out, and unless he found the hidden object, his days at FLETC could be ending. Confident there was nothing in her pants, he concluded the only possibility was the woman's bra.

Devin tried not to make eye contact with the woman as she stood there with her legs spread and her arms straight out to her sides. He noticed his classmates staring at him, wondering how he would handle searching the woman's bra in front of the entire class. It would have been easier if she had a shirt on over the bra, but there she stood, in front of everyone, wearing nothing but a B cup brassiere.

At this point, it was hard to tell who was more embarrassed— the female role player, allowing herself to be groped by a stranger, or Devin, hesitant to do anything that might be considered inappropriate. He knew there was a fine line between conducting a thorough search and accidentally exposing the woman's breast in front of the entire class. Devin looked to the instructor for guidance, but none came. He sighed, knowing what he had to do. Suddenly, the woman cut her eyes toward him and whispered, "Just do what you gotta do."

Devin slowly walked behind the woman, reached up from behind, and got a hand full of B-cup. He quickly maneuvered his hand to feel for any foreign object but found nothing. He then moved to her left breast. Time was running out, and he hadn't found the contraband. He looked composed, but internally, he was in full panic mode. He knew he might have to pull her breast out of her bra to search before time expired.

As he reached around to check her left breast, he felt nothing at first. Then, as his fingertips touched the wire at the bottom of the bra, he thought he felt something that shouldn't be there. Without looking directly at her, he lifted the bottom of her bra, and a small syringe fell to the floor. Devin passed the exam, realizing just how close he had come to failing. He hadn't felt the syringe through the bra and was not familiar with the wire at the bottom; it was luck that he checked the exact spot where the contraband was hidden.

Although relieved to have passed the exam, there were still several weeks left until the course was completed. Each day after training, Devin and his teammates—those who sat at connected tables and were grouped alphabetically—met in their dormitory's game room to study for upcoming exams. He studied more in the two months of CITP than he had in four years of high school.

At the beginning of their training, the class was given an investigation to solve by the cadre. Every practical skill they were taught related to this overall investigation, culminating at the end of their training. Each witness interview and search warrant they conducted during their evaluation led them closer to the criminal mastermind, "Sturgeon."

During the last week of training, the team had enough information to execute the arrest warrant for Sturgeon. They planned how to assault his home, geared up, and headed to the shoot houses to make the arrest. The shoot houses were always fun, but dangerous. The trainees were armed with simunitions and often engaged in gunfights with the training instructors hidden throughout the houses. By this time, the team was ready. They had uncovered enough evidence against Sturgeon to prosecute him. All they needed to do was arrest him and get his confession.

The team pulled up to Sturgeon's house in three vehicles and stacked up at the front door. Devin's friend Paul was at the front of the line, and Devin was second. The door was locked, so they called for the ram to break the latch. As the door flew open, the trainees flooded the room. Paul and Devin stormed in and immediately froze; there was Sturgeon sitting in a lazy-boy chair getting a lap dance from a role player pretending to be a stripper, wearing only a bra and fishnet stockings. Devin, unprepared for this scenario, froze. The rest of the team poured in behind him, assuming their positions while he and Paul argued over who would search the stripper.

The plan was for Paul to search the first person they encountered, followed by Devin. When they saw the stripper sitting on top of Sturgeon, it wasn't clear who should search whom. As the rest of the team continued down the hallway, Devin and Paul remained in the front room, arguing. Both men yelled, "Put your hands up! Put your hands up!"

Paul shouted to the woman, "Come over here, put your hands up!" only for Devin to counter, "No, come over here. Show me your hands!" The female and Sturgeon were confused, unsure whose direction to follow. While Devin and Paul gave conflicting commands, the rest of the team got "annihilated" by the instructors in the remaining rooms. After the instructors called an end to the exercise, Paul and Devin laughed at each other in the front room, only to see their teammates covered in paint from the simunitions. Devin and Paul quickly realized their foolishness had caused the rest of their team to fail the exercise and put their graduation in jeopardy.

After a stern berating from the cadre, the team was given one more chance to pass the exam. This time, they had to execute a search warrant on a suspect known to have weapons inside his home. The instructor addressed the team one last time before the exercise began.

"Listen up, guys. You failed this exercise because you didn't work together as a team. This is your last chance. If you fail again, you'll be dismissed, and you won't graduate. It all comes down to this. Remember your training, look out for each other, shoot, move, and communicate. Now let's go."

The team drove up in their unmarked cars and stacked up at the house. They entered and cleared the first room, the kitchen, then stacked up to go down the hallway. Devin was last in line. The team moved forward, but Devin stayed back in the kitchen to cover their rear. As the team advanced through the house, they missed searching a small laundry room. Two instructors exited the laundry room to ambush the team.

Devin saw the instructors and quickly took their place inside the laundry room. Once inside the small room, he called out the ambush to his team. They immediately began firing on the instructors, who tried to retreat to the laundry room where Devin was waiting for them. He fired two shots, filling both of their visors with paint and successfully ending the exercise.

Although the team was relieved about finishing the test, Devin felt embarrassed because he had let his team down. All he could think about was, *What if this was a real situation and I got distracted? My whole team would be dead, and it would be my fault.*

The final PT test was scheduled for the next afternoon. The temperature was in the high nineties, prompting the instructors to consider rescheduling the test for the following morning. However, almost the entire class voted to proceed despite the heat so they would not have to get up two hours earlier the next day. As with almost every other run, Devin finished near the back of the pack. His teammates didn't understand why he struggled so much with the distance running, especially since he appeared to be in excellent physical condition. Devin had excelled in defensive tactics training, arrest techniques, and maneuvering through the shoot houses.

What his classmates didn't know was that Devin had a torn ACL in his right knee. It had been torn before he arrived at FLETC, and all the running made his knee swell up to twice its normal size. On most days, Devin had a tough time walking between classes, as the main classroom was about a mile from his dormitory. Yet, he was determined to make it through without complaining about his knee pain, fearing he would be kicked out if he did. His perseverance paid off, and after completing the CITP, he went on to graduate from the Basic Special Investigations Course at the OSI Academy.

Two weeks after becoming a credential federal agent, Devin arrived at the OSI detachment at Tyndall Air Force Base, outside of Panama City, Florida, for his first assignment as a Special Agent. He was greeted by the detachment Commander and the Superintendent, both of whom seemed to be laid-back family men. The agents of the detachment were noticeably young, with half of them having less than a year's experience as agents. Devin was quickly informed that he would be taking over as the on-call "duty agent" on Friday, but he was assured that nothing usually happened.

After being issued his weapon and ammunition, the reality of realizing his dream began to sink in. The first week of his twelve-month probationary period was mostly uneventful, filled with paperwork and ancillary training. Finally, the weekend arrived.

On Saturday morning, Devin was in his apartment watching television when the phone rang.

"Hello, this is the Tyndall Law Enforcement Desk. I am notifying you of an active-duty death."

Devin was so nervous that he did not immediately respond.

"Hello, Agent Jackson, are you there?" asked the desk operator.

"Yes, I'm here. Can you please repeat what you just said?"

This time, Devin wrote down what the operator said and quickly called Agent Danison from the detachment. He explained that an Air Force Major had just been pronounced dead by the Bay County Coroner. Two hours later, the agents met up at the coroner's office to attend the autopsy. Devin was so nervous he was almost visibly shaking.

"I can't believe how fast they're getting to the autopsy. They must be really slow right now," said Danison as he and Devin walked into the coroner's office. A representative from the Sheriff's Office met them inside and escorted them to the autopsy room where the coroner was waiting.

"Good afternoon, gentlemen. If you guys are ready, I'd like to go ahead and begin."

Devin and Danison stood on the side of the table as the coroner opened the decedent's chest cavity. Within minutes, the coroner had removed the heart and its valves for inspection. Seemingly knowing exactly where to look, the coroner pointed out a clogged artery he believed could have been the cause of death. Danison, obviously more experienced, stood close to the table and leaned over to inspect the body. Devin stood at least five feet behind him, praying they would not ask him for assistance.

When the agents returned to the office on Monday, everyone laughed at Devin's luck for being assigned a death investigation during his first week on the job. The detachment superintendent followed Devin to his office and discussed the next few steps of the investigation, which included interviewing the Major's wife. The superintendent assured Devin that he would not be thrown to the wolves and that Agent Charlton would assist him during the interview.

Two days later, on Wednesday night, Devin and Agent Charlton arrived at the Major's home. They rang the doorbell, and a woman in her early thirties came to the door. When it opened, Devin quickly recognized that the woman was several months pregnant. All he could think was that the situation had gone from bad to extremely bad very quickly. Mrs. Donovan invited the agents into her living room to have a seat. Then there was silence; Agent Charlton did not say a word, and Mrs. Donovan stared at them, expecting an explanation about the latest findings of the investigation.

Feeling the awkwardness of the moment, Devin expressed remorse for the loss of her husband and explained that he needed to gather background information that could be used to determine the cause of her husband's death.

Mrs. Donovan suddenly became emotional, explaining her fear of having to raise her child without a father. Devin struggled to get a word in between her crying outbursts, while Agent Charlton continued to sit silently on the couch. Finally, Mrs. Donovan explained that her family had recently moved to Florida from an airbase in Germany.

"Mrs. Donovan, we won't know the exact cause of your husband's death until the coroner releases his report, but there are some questions I need to ask that may assist in his determination. Was your husband taking any drugs or prescription medication?" Devin asked.

Mrs. Donovan, steadily wiping away tears and blowing her nose, replied, "No, he didn't use any drugs, and he wasn't on any prescription medication…but I did give him some of my pills."

Devin shot a glance at Agent Charlton, who finally seemed to wake from his daze. "You gave him some of your pills? What kind of pills?" Devin asked.

"Wait, why are you asking me that? Do you think I killed my husband? Do you think I actually killed my own husband?" Mrs. Donovan shouted, falling into a grief-stricken fit of screaming and crying. Agent Charlton remained quiet on the couch as the widow berated Devin for his insinuation.

Devin responded, "No, ma'am, I'm not saying you did anything to your husband, but I need to know what type of pills you gave him to determine whether he had a reaction to the medication. What did you give him?"

"How dare you suggest that I killed my husband! I let you in my house, and this is what you do to me?" She cried uncontrollably. Devin felt himself sinking lower into the couch. He looked over to Charlton, who appeared to be watching the drama play out like it was his favorite soap opera. Realizing he was on his own, Devin found the courage to continue the questioning.

"Mrs. Donovan, what pills did you give your husband?"

"I gave him my pain pills!" she screamed back. "The doctor in Germany prescribed me pain medication for my menstrual cramps. My husband was complaining that his neck had been hurting for several days, so I gave him my pills, and he took them. He kept complaining that his neck was hurting, so I drove him to the emergency room. He was lying down in the back seat, and I looked back and noticed he had turned blue. I pulled over and called 911, but he was gone by the time they arrived. Are you satisfied, Agent Jackson?"

Feeling about an inch tall, Devin hurriedly concluded the interview. "Yes ma'am, that's all I needed. Do you still have the pill bottle?"

"Are you kidding me?" Mrs. Donovan stormed out of the room and returned with a half-empty bottle of pain pills. She handed the bottle to Agent Charlton. Devin rose to his feet, indicating that the interview was over. Mrs. Donovan cordially escorted the agents to the door.

On the way back to the base, Devin was extremely furious with Agent Charlton for not helping to comfort Mrs. Donovan or assist with the interview. "Well, I don't think she was happy to speak with us," Devin said.

Charlton responded, "Yeah, you get 'em like that sometimes." Devin looked at Charlton side-eyed and promised himself he would never trust him again.

Like most agents during their probationary year, Devin struggled to manage his time wisely. While the investigative work started to make sense, the overwhelming amount of paperwork caused a lot of headaches. The majority of his time was spent not on investigations but on managing the weapons program, which included overseeing the guns and ammunition for the detachment.

Devin also struggled to feel natural in his position. Wearing suits to work was not a problem, but the 'pro casual' dress code was a huge obstacle. As the only Black agent in the office, he tried to match the attire of his co-workers, but it made him feel like a clown. It wasn't that there was anything wrong with their clothes; it just wasn't natural for Devin. Sometimes he would walk past a mirror and shake his head, convinced that everyone else must have thought the same thing: that he looked corny.

Three months into his assignment, while visiting the Law Enforcement desk, Devin requested information on Master Sergeant Bowe regarding a rash of stolen motorcycles in base housing. Bowe was a flight chief with the Security Forces Squadron, and Devin was shocked to learn that he had been arrested by the Panama City Beach Police Department for slamming an officer down on the hood of his vehicle. "How is this guy not in jail?" Devin said aloud as he reviewed Bowe's background. Devin began to call and email Master Sgt. Bowe to schedule an interview to determine whether he had knowledge about the burglaries occurring in base housing.

Approximately six months into his probationary period, around the beginning of March, Devin was the "Duty Agent" for the week and was locking up the office when he got an email from the Region Chief informing him he had been selected for a twelve-month remote assignment to Osan Airbase in South Korea. He drove home distracted, not only by the upcoming move overseas but also by the next steps in the theft investigation. About an hour after he arrived home, he received a call from the Law Enforcement Desk.

"Agent Jackson, we have a lady here at the L.E. desk who says her teenage daughter was brought onto the base and was raped by two airmen."

"Okay, tell her to stay at the visitor's center. I'll be there in twenty minutes."

Devin hung up the phone and called Agent Xander. Normally, he would have called a more senior agent to help him, but Agent Xander had graduated from the academy about a month prior and had yet to be involved in a meaningful interview. About a half-hour later, Devin and Xander arrived at the base visitor center and greeted the mother, who was standing outside her minivan. The woman, an African American who appeared to be in her early fifties, was visibly shaken by what had happened to her daughter.

"My daughter told me she met two guys at McDonald's who brought her back to the dormitory on base, and they raped her," the mother said. The emotional weight of the moment made it extremely hard for her to speak. "This happened to me twenty years ago. I got raped, and I never wanted any of my children to go through that."

Devin thanked the woman for speaking to him and asked for permission to speak to her daughter. The mother told the agents her daughter was eighteen years old and that she was sitting in the back of the minivan.

Devin, nervous about the mental and physical state he might find the girl in, slid the door open on the vehicle and saw the girl sitting in the seat, curled up into a ball and covering herself with a blanket. She was crying inconsolably, which made the mother even more emotional. Devin tried to talk to the girl, but she wouldn't speak. He turned back to the mother. "Ma'am, we need to get you both back to our office. Please follow me through the gate, and then we'll get started with the interview."

The woman agreed and followed the agents back to the detachment. As they walked into the lobby, the daughter was so emotional she could barely walk, continually screaming out for her mother's help. Agent Xander grew nervous, realizing this interview could be extremely invasive. Devin tried to speak to the daughter in the lobby, but she wouldn't communicate and continued to cry and cling to her mother.

Devin and Xander decided they needed to separate the girl from her mother, as the mother's emotions seemed to trigger the victim. Devin explained the situation to the mother, who agreed to wait patiently in the lobby while the agents took her daughter to be interviewed.

Devin led the girl to the interview room and took a seat a few feet in front of her, while Xander sat at a desk in the corner to take notes. Devin began by asking simple questions to help the girl relax and earn her trust. As soon as the questioning started, her entire demeanor changed. She was no longer squeezing herself tightly with her arms, and her tears had dried up. After the initial background questions were answered, Devin decided it was time to get her account of the sexual assault.

As Devin moved his chair a bit closer to the girl, he said, "Hey, I know this is probably a bit scary for you, but we're here to help. If somebody did something to you, we need to know about it so they can be held accountable and to make sure they never do this again to anyone else."

By this time, most of the girl's defensive barriers had disappeared, and she began to tell her story. "I was at the McDonald's right outside the base when these two guys came in and started talking to me. They said they were in the Air Force and asked if I wanted to come back to their dorm and listen to some music. I said, yeah, okay, and got in their car, and we went to their room. Everything was cool at first, then they started giving me alcohol. I don't know exactly what it was, but it made me really sleepy."

"Hold up!" Devin interrupted. "So, there were two guys in the room? How did they force you to drink the alcohol?"

"Well, they didn't really force me to drink it. They just kept pressuring me. So, I started drinking, and I got sleepy. I remember they kept rubbing my back while I was drinking and sitting on the bed."

"Okay, did you have sex with just one of them or both?" Devin asked.

"I don't know. I don't know if I had sex, but I feel like something happened."

Devin paused as he was confused by the girl's answer, "What do you mean, you feel like something happened? Did you have sex or not?"

"See, that's the thing. The alcohol made me tired, and I fell asleep on the bed. When I woke up, I couldn't see because I had this stuff on my face, so I went and washed my face in the toilet."

Agent Xander slowly looked up from his notes to signal to Devin that he needed to continue with his questioning. Devin understood Xander's concerns and pressed forward with the interview.

"Wait, what did you say? You washed your face in the toilet?"

"Yeah, I had to. I had this stuff all over my face, and I couldn't see, so I washed my face in the toilet," the girl answered.

Devin, only a few months out of the academy, was still used to interviews with role players who gave very generic and scientific answers provided by the instructors.

Devin knew the girl was referring to ejaculate on her face, but he needed her to say specifically what it was. "So what was on your face that you had to wash off?"

The girl looked at Devin as though he was the dumbest person she'd ever met in her life and then responded, "It was nut!"

Devin sharply looked down at the floor, holding his breath to avoid laughing uncontrollably. He took a quick peek at Agent Xander, who was staring at him as though he were about to witness a car wreck. Devin noticed the girl watching his reaction and quickly turned away. He couldn't speak, and his body started shaking from his attempts to hold in his laughter. After about five seconds, which felt like five minutes, Devin could no longer hold it and let out a loud chuckle. He immediately caught himself and held his breath again as the young lady stared at him.

At this point, Devin's shaking had become uncontrollable, and he let out another loud "Ha ha." He knew this was completely inappropriate, but he couldn't stop laughing. He even covered his mouth with his hand, but it only made things worse. Even though he was laughing, Devin was terrified because he realized he was laughing at a teenage rape victim directly in her face! The hand covering his mouth didn't work, and Devin laughed aloud. He couldn't stop! As the giggling continued, Devin thought, "Oh my God, I'm gonna get fired!" However, the laughing continued.

The teenage girl sat up in her chair, trying to come to grips with what was happening as Devin, sitting less than five feet in front of her, laughed at her words. She looked over to Agent Xander for clarification. Xander, with a humongous smile on his face, realized what had triggered Devin but managed to hold it together. The girl turned back to Devin, who was still laughing, completely embarrassed by what had happened. Suddenly, the girl joined in and burst into laughter. Within moments, Xander joined in, and the interview room sounded like a late-night comedy club.

As the girl continued to laugh, Devin finally regained his composure. He apologized to Agent Xander for causing the awkward situation. Not sure if Xander would inform the Detachment Superintendent, Devin waited for the butt chewing, but it never came

The next day, the agents interviewed the two airmen who had brought the girl onto the base. As expected, both denied committing the assault, but one of them mentioned that he had made a video on his phone. The agents seized the phone and downloaded the data onto a disk for storage in evidence.

What followed was an uncomfortable conversation with the girl's mother. The agents had to inform her that her daughter had not been raped but was an active participant in the sexual activity. The scene in the video matched the girl's description, except she was fully awake, and no one was forcing her to participate. The mother was embarrassed to learn that her daughter had lied to her but relieved that she had not been raped, even though her actions did not represent her family well.

A few weeks later, as Devin was returning to the office from lunch, he was greeted by another agent who was leaving. "Hey man, there's somebody waiting for you in the interview room."

"For me? Who is it?"

"I think he said his name was Bowe."

"Crap, that's the guy who slammed the cop on top of his car downtown." Devin was not prepared for this type of interview, but it didn't matter—it was happening. He looked around the office and grabbed Agent Xander to take notes during the interview. Devin walked in and found Bowe pacing the room like a heavyweight boxer waiting for his opponent.

"Are you Special Agent Jackson?"

"Yes, I've been trying to reach—"

"I don't care what you've been trying to do. You keep calling my house, calling my job, leaving me voicemails, and now you've got my job on my back about talking to you."

"Master Sgt. Bowe, calm down. I just wanted to—"

"I don't care what you wanted to do. I didn't do anything! What you wanna do, Devin?"

Within the first thirty seconds, Devin realized this would not be a normal interview. He had every intention of questioning Bowe as a potential witness, but now Bowe was inches from his face in full combat mode. Devin took a glance over at Xander who sat frozen in his seat, afraid to make eye contact with Bowe. Everything about Bowe's body language suggested he was moments away from attacking, so Devin went on the offensive. The two men yelled at each other at the top of the lungs for the next fifteen minutes.

The lone female agent in the detachment was watching the video feed and thought the two men were about to fight each other. She ran to tell the detachment superintendent, who initially disregarded her concerns.

Back in the interview room, Bowe and Devin continued screaming at each other. Devin, convinced it would become physical at any moment, forgot where he was and handled the situation as though he was on the street, about to fight a guy much larger than he was. Suddenly, there was a loud bang as the superintendent kicked the door open.

"Sit your ass down! Right now!" he yelled at Bowe. "DJ, I need to talk to you in the hallway."

Devin turned around to see his boss's face and was instantly pulled back to reality. *Oh crap, I'm getting fired*, he thought. Devin followed the superintendent into the hallway and closed the door, absolutely sure he was about to get a world-class butt-chewing and preparing himself to turn in his badge for losing his composure.

"DJ, you alright?" the superintendent asked.

"Yeah, I'm good," Devin replied.

"Good job. Keep it up," the superintendent said before turning and walking back to his office.

The positive reinforcement caught Devin off guard, and he stood in the hallway for a moment before returning to the interview. As soon as he walked back through the door, Master Sgt. Bowe apologized for losing his temper.

"Man, I just wanted to ask you if you've seen any of these missing motorcycles," Devin said.

Master Sgt. Bowe laughed. "That's all, man? I thought you were going to accuse me of stealing all this shit!"

The two men laughed and continued with the interview.

Over the next three months, Devin continued to work on his theft investigation but was unable to solve the case. His limited experience prevented him from blending what he felt needed to be done with what OSI expected and allowed him to do. As his time at Tyndall ended, he transferred the investigation over to Security Forces Investigations and prepared for his tour in Korea.

CHAPTER 3
ANNYEONGHASEYO

The first week in August

Devin's plane arrived at Osan Airbase in the Pyeongtaek Province of South Korea. As soon as he stepped off the plane, the smell of cow manure pierced his nostrils so strongly that he wished for another twelve-hour flight to get him away from there. Devin gathered his belongings at the terminal and was met by two local agents who brought him to OSI Detachment 611. Although he still had two months left on his probationary period, Devin was assigned to lead black market investigations.

On his first Sunday at Osan, Devin attended the gospel service at the base chapel. It was full of people, and they all seemed to be having an exciting time. The choir sounded as though they had been singing together for years, and the congregation included everyone he had seen in the club the night before. Midway through the service, an official up front was reading the church announcements and asked all first-time visitors to stand and introduce themselves by telling where they came from and their newly assigned unit. About ten people stood, made introductions, and were welcomed with loud applause from the congregation. Devin stood and was handed the microphone.

"Good morning, my name is Devin Jackson. I just arrived here from Tyndall Air Force Base, and I'm assigned to OSI."

That was a mistake. Instantly, the chapel was filled with loud gasps and laughter as everyone turned their backs to him. Some even began covering their faces. The official reading the announcements stuttered and struggled to get the congregation to quiet back down. Devin stood there, confused about why the people responded that way. Over the next twelve months, he would earn that reaction.

During his tour, Devin and the other agents assigned to Osan were worked to the point of exhaustion with the number of sexual assault investigations that seem to be reported like clockwork. The agents got accustomed to working over twenty-four-hour shifts because there were only four of them assigned to the criminal investigations branch, and several of the assaults required immediate searches to gather evidence. After a few months in Korea, Devin began to feel more relaxed and gained confidence in his abilities. Little did he or his partners know that all hell was about to break loose.

It was around 2130 hours, and the base hospital was closed for the night. Most of the office lights had been turned off except for the areas being cleaned by the janitors. Inside the pharmacy, two Air Force members, Technical Sergeant Wilson and Staff Sergeant Ramirez, were moving about in their civilian clothing. The two men used flashlights as they carefully emptied pills out of the bottles and into small plastic bags. They were careful not to completely empty the bottles, taking only a few pills from each container.

A few miles away, Air Force Special Agent Al Sparks, dressed in his black leather jacket, jeans, and Timberland boots, was walking through the entertainment district in Songtan, located immediately outside of Osan Airbase. Sparks, a six-foot tall, dark-skinned brother who tilted his cap slightly to the east, looked like he would rather be in the gym than any other place on earth. He had been assigned to Osan for about six weeks but had been an agent at Little Rock Air Force Base for the previous two years. Sparks appeared popular among the Air Force personnel in the area, as several people greeted him as he walked past. But as usual, not everyone had a good relationship with law enforcement, especially Black law enforcement, and Sparks noticed a few people looked his way and quickly left the area. This was not a recent occurrence, so he continued to a local sports bar where he was greeted by his co-worker, Air Force Special Agent Zachary, who was waiting to order dinner.

Agent Zachary, mostly called Zach by the other agents, was dressed very conservatively, looking like a typical off-duty cop in hiking boots, cargo pants, and a polo shirt. The red-headed agent was in his early thirties and sported a semi-military haircut.

Although their backgrounds were completely different, Sparks and Zach quickly became good friends. Sparks, raised by a Jamaican immigrant mother, had family ties to Florida but mostly grew up in Connecticut. His street savvy made him an expert drug agent and informant handler. He loved OSI's mission but could not care less for its bureaucracy. Zach was OSI's version of the prototypical agent. He grew up in the Midwest, had multiple deployments under his belt, and was a tactical genius. Agent Zachary outworked and out-studied everyone else, excelling at just about every task except blending into the streets. However, spending time with Sparks and Devin would soon change that.

Sitting inside the sports bar, Sparks and Zach reviewed the menu and were trying to decide what to order when the waitress approached. She was a Filipino woman, wearing a short miniskirt and a halter top. The waitress greeted the two agents and asked if they were ready to order.

"Yeah, I'll have the chicken tenders and fries with a coke," Sparks replied.

Zachary ordered a cheeseburger combo with a Sprite. The waitress wrote down their orders and headed to the kitchen. A few minutes later, she returned with their food, and the men enjoyed their meals while watching a soccer game on the television.

As they were eating, Wilson and Ramirez entered the restaurant and headed straight for the bar. The waitress saw them and appeared to shy away. The bar owner emerged from the kitchen and led Wilson into a back room. Wilson cautiously pulled out a plastic bag full of pills and handed it to the bar owner, who then gave Wilson an envelope full of cash. While Wilson conducted business in the back, Ramirez sat at the bar, harassing any waitress bold enough to walk past him. Wilson exited the back room with a look of invincibility. He nodded toward Ramirez, and the two men left the restaurant.

Feeling a bit more secure after Ramirez left the bar, the waitress returned to the agents' table and sat down next to Zachary. She waved for another waitress to come and sit next to Sparks, and both waitresses became very flirtatious.

"Do you have a girlfriend?" the waitress asked Zachary.

"Me? Nah, I'm a single man. No girlfriends yet," Zach responded.

Sparks laughed as Zachary appeared completely uncomfortable with the waitress rubbing her hands over his shoulders and chest. Then the waitress turned to Sparks. "What about you? You got a girlfriend?" She leaned over and tried to kiss Sparks, but he pushed her face away.

"Okay, time to go," said Sparks, motioning for Zachary to get up from the table. As Zachary stood, the waitress pulled on his clothing.

"Hey, where are you going? I want to go with you. Please, I need the money."

"Yeah, that's not gonna happen." Zachary pulled the woman's hands off his shirt and moved to leave the bar.

Sparks was still laughing at Zachary when the ajeema, an older Korean woman who helped manage the restaurant, approached him and asked for money to take the waitress home with him. "What about you? You take girl tonight?"

Sparks briefly looked over to the waitress, who was missing her bottom teeth, and shook his head. "What kind of freaky restaurant is this? All I wanted was some damn chicken tenders!" Sparks and Zachary managed to break free from the waitress's grip and laughed their way out of the restaurant.

Two alleys away from where the agents had dinner, an unsuspecting building fit in perfectly with the surrounding structures. On the second floor was another sports bar frequented by service members. This night was no different, as the bar was half full of patrons playing pool, throwing darts, and indulging in the Korean soju. None of them had reason to know that only one floor above them were young women, locked in cages, being held as victims of human trafficking.

On the third floor, in the dimly lit warehouse storage facility, a young Filipino woman was sweating and desperately trying to release herself from her shackles. After maneuvering her small arms through her constraints, she found that the cage she was housed in was not locked. She slowly pushed the door open, stepped out onto the floor, and walked toward the only light she saw, which was coming from the exit to the fire escape.

The young girl was terrified, as she had no idea where she was, and her vision was still blurry from being drugged when she arrived in Korea. She slowly made her way down the fire escape to the second floor, opened the door, and walked inside. The music in the bar was blasting, and a few people on the dance floor were spilling their drinks as they tried to show off their skills. Suddenly, the side door opened, and the Filipino woman from the third floor walked into the bar, barefoot. The music stopped, and everyone turned to see what was happening.

The confused girl walked up to a waitress and asked for help, but she was quickly reprimanded. "You're not supposed to be here. You're not supposed to be here!!" The waitress was terrified, and she slowly looked to the corner of the room where an older white male was sitting alone, smoking a cigarette. The man, Viktor Kovalenko, was still wearing his suit from work and often frequented the bars outside of Osan. Kovalenko saw what was unfolding and slowly turned away in disgust. He turned to the bar owner, who stood motionless, almost petrified by what had happened. Kovalenko then gave a quick nod to the owner to hurry and manage the situation.

A couple of GIs walked up to the girl to see if she was alright. The bar owner, afraid of the questions that might come his way, quickly brushed the Americans away. "She's fine, she's fine," said the owner. "Everything is okay. She's just lost. I will help her. Please, go back to your drinks."

The bar owner grabbed the girl by her shoulders and turned her around to walk her back out of the bar. As soon as the door closed behind them, he slapped the girl's face. "How did you get out? You're not supposed to be here!" He dragged her back upstairs and threw her into her cage. He caught sight of the bowl of rice he left out for her hours earlier and noticed that she had not eaten it. Angrily, he kicked the bowl toward her and walked away, laughing.

The owner headed back to the exit to return to the bar. As soon as he walked out onto the fire escape, Kovalenko slammed him back against the building and punched him in the abdomen multiple times. Kovalenko pulled the owner's hair back, lifted his chin, and placed a four-inch blade to the man's throat. Leaning in close to ensure the owner knew who was assaulting him, he said, "You worthless bitch! I can't trust you for shit! That girl weighs ninety pounds. Tell me how she was able to get out of her chains. Look, I got a lot of money tied up in this business, and I'm not too keen on losing it because some slant-eyed piece of shit like you forgot to lock the door. If you screw up again, that's your ass!"

The next morning, Devin arrived at the Osan courtroom to testify in a court-martial for a sexual assault case. Feeling more comfortable in his role, Devin no longer had issues with work attire. Songan had a plethora of tailors who provided custom-made suits, and Devin took full advantage of their resources. He paced back and forth in the lobby, as this was his first time testifying in one of his own investigations. Suddenly, the tall wooden doors swung open, and Devin was signaled to enter the courtroom.

Devin walked up to the witness stand and did his best to display confidence as he was sworn in. The prosecutor asked

Devin if he could identify the suspect, at which point Devin happily pointed to him sitting beside his defense counsel. The first few questions were a breeze, as Devin was asked to describe his background and education. As the questioning continued, the prosecutor asked Devin how he was sure the suspect broke into the victim's dorm room.

Devin replied, "As I was interviewing the subject, he denied having broken into the victim's room. However, my co-worker, Special Agent Sparks, was at the crime scene at that very moment and discovered footprints outside her window. It appeared that whoever climbed through the window stepped down onto her laptop, leaving their shoe print on the computer. I was called out of the interview and informed of the design of that print. I then went back into the interview and asked to see the bottom of the subject's shoe. His response was, 'Yeah, these are the shoes I had on when I climbed through the window.' With that statement, not only did he confess to breaking and entering, but it also confirmed that the victim did not invite him into her room, and he had been lying to federal agents for the previous two hours."

The defense attorney looked down at his papers, knowing the eventual outcome of the case would not be in his client's favor.

After leaving the courtroom, Devin returned to the detachment. He stopped by the gun safe to retrieve his Sig, and as usual, he messed up the combination on his first try but managed to get the vault open the second time around. He reached in with his right hand to pull out the weapon and grabbed three magazines with his left. After loading his pistol, Devin walked back to the bullpen, the section in the rear of the office with four cubicles, two conjoined on each side, and met with Sparks, Zachary, and Detective Kim, a twenty-six-year-old Korean female on liaison assignment from the Korean National Police.

Also, in the bullpen, dressed in the day's uniform, was the office manager, twenty-five-year-old Staff Sergeant Ella Mae Stringer. She was the youngest member of the detachment but proved to be irreplaceable because she took care of the evidence and contingency funds, in addition to her normal administrative duties. Ella was a light-skinned sister with braids who loved to experiment with new hairstyles. Her desk was located down the hallway, closer to the lobby door. She had been trying to get Devin's attention for a few weeks, but she did not want to seem overaggressive and destroy their team dynamics. So, every now and then, she would drop subtle hints, but Devin was so engaged with the investigations that he failed to recognize her efforts and only saw her as everyone else did—the 'little sister' of the detachment.

Ella Mae was absolutely in love with anime and considered her assignment to OSI the thrill of a lifetime, particularly because she loved watching crime movies and police reality TV shows. Sometimes she listened so intently during case discussions that some agents thought she might be authoring a book based on their investigations. However, there was no book—just a young woman who was surrounded by her heroes, who turned out to be her best friends.

Devin strutted through the hallway and into the bullpen. "What's up, fellas?"

Sparks and Zach quickly returned the greeting to Devin, but Ella Mae saw it as an opportunity to start trouble. "Oh, so I'm just one of the fellas?"

"Do you wanna be one of the fellas?"

Ella paused for a second. "Yeah, kinda, but I mean, not really."

Before Devin could respond, Agent Mullins, the detachment superintendent, yelled his name. "Jackson! Bring me all your case files. I need to do a monthly review."

As usual, Devin jumped a little at the sound of Mullins's screeching voice and instantly felt flustered.

"What's wrong, man?" Sparks asked.

"My case files are jacked up! I've been so busy with these interviews I haven't had time to organize them," said Devin.

Sparks took the moment to assert his "big brother" role. "Yeah, man, you gotta stay on top of that. Zach will tell you; Mullins don't play around with that stuff. You just gotta make time to organize your work."

Although they hadn't known each other for long, Sparks was the mentor Devin needed. Often, Devin had ideas to help his investigations but lacked the know-how to get it done. Sparks had the answer: just get up and do it.

Devin stood up from his desk and grabbed his case files to do a quick cleanup before heading to Mullins's office. There were a couple of loose papers stuffed inside. He walked the files down to Mullins's office and sat them on her desk before walking back to the bullpen with a worried look on his face.

"Now you know that's a shame!" exclaimed Ella Mae, and she laughed at Devin's predicament.

"Dang, DJ, was it that bad?" Zachary asked.

Devin shrugged. "I guess we'll find out soon enough."

Zach interrupted Devin's pity party by bringing up what happened at the sports bar the previous night. "Bro, I was trying to pay the bill. Next thing you know, she was trying to put her hands down my pants."

Everyone in the office laughed except Detective Kim. "This prostitution issue goes deeper than you realize."

"Oh yeah, well, she went pretty deep down my pants last night," Zachary joked.

Always one to find a way to play a joke on Zach, Ella Mae chimed in. "Were you wearing boxers or briefs?"

Zach was stunned. Like everyone else in the detachment, he never knew when Ella was joking or being serious. The group was in the middle of a huge laugh when the detachment commander, Agent Chang, walked back to the bullpen.

"Agent Zachary, you won't believe this, but your story is perfect timing. The Wing Commander just tasked me yesterday with gathering more information about prostitution right outside of the gate. Apparently, a lot of young airmen have gotten into financial troubles, and they're saying they're spending all their money on 'juicy girls'."

Zach shook his head. "That girl last night didn't look juicy to me at all."

Interrupting the conversation, Agent Mullins called Devin back to her office. "Hey, Devin, I've got a tasker for you."

"Yeah, the boss just told us about the prostitution."

"Prostitution? Nah, don't worry about that. Let Zach handle that. I need you to take lead on our drug investigations."

Devin was instantly concerned about this direction as he had just finished his probationary time. He'd never managed any drug investigations at Tyndall. He sat for a second, searching for a way out of the assignment. He thought he had found one. "Okay, I don't really have a lot of experience with that, but you know, Sparks ran the JDET at his last detachment. Maybe he'll be a better fit. Plus, I'm already taking lead on the black market cases."

Mullins was not happy with Devin's response. "Look, you knew this job would be challenging when you signed up for it. The team is counting on you. And by the way, where are we with the black market?"

Devin realized he had dug himself a deeper hole. "So, yeah, I probably shouldn't have mentioned that, huh? I'll be honest with you. I'm not sure what you're expecting with that. I mean, we found people selling uniforms off base that were stolen from the BX, but you weren't interested in that. Correct me if I'm wrong, but you want us chasing after hot dog thieves?"

Agent Mullins, delighted in the opportunity to knock Devin down a peg or two, closed the case files and crossed her legs.

"Agent Jackson, as I've told you before, food that is sold at the Commissary and Shoppette is shipped over here only for the benefit of service members and their families. If someone's wife, who happens to be Korean, then sells that food off base to her family's restaurant, then, well, that's fraud, and the service member can and will be prosecuted under the UCMJ. Got it?"

Devin nodded. "Yeah, I got it, but it seems like a waste of time."

"I don't care what it seems like to you. Just get it done!"

Feeling a bit overwhelmed, Devin returned to his desk and informed Zach and Sparks of Mullins's decision to place him in charge of all drug investigations.

Noticing the look of uncertainty on Devin's face, Sparks offered his help in getting started. Agent Zachary overheard the conversation and chimed in.

"Hey, you know what? Somebody from the base pharmacy called the office the other day asking about the biological threat in South Korea. It sounded like they were trying to make sure they had the right vaccines on hand."

Showing his inexperience, Devin looked at Zachary like a confused puppy. "Why would I want to know about biological weapons?"

Sparks laughed at Devin's moment of ignorance. "Nah, man, if he works at the pharmacy, maybe he can give us a heads up about people trying to abuse their prescriptions. I mean, it's a start, right?"

"Oh…yeah, that'll work. Let's hit him up tomorrow," Devin replied.

Before Sparks could respond, Agent Chang walked back into the bullpen and gave Sparks some unexpected news. "Sparks, pack your bags. I need to send you to Busan for a couple of days. Agent Yang needs help with a sexual assault case. I'm sorry for the last-minute notice, but I need you there by tomorrow night."

Excited about the three-hour trip to the fast-paced city, Sparks easily accepted his assignment. "Busan it is. Yang's a cool dude anyway."

As Agent Chang walked back to his office, Sparks leaned over Devin's desk to adjust their plans. "DJ, if we're gonna hit up the pharmacy, it's got to be today."

"Whenever you're ready," Devin replied.

As the agents prepared to leave the office, a loud, obnoxious yell filled the office. Agent Mullins was back on the prowl.

"Sparks! Bring me your case files!"

Devin, Zachary, and Ella Mae slowly turned toward Sparks, waiting for his reaction. Sparks, already aware of the disarray in his case files, had been hoping to make it to Busan without completing the monthly review. When Agent Mullins shouted his name, Sparks's face fell. With a heavy sigh, he trudged over to the cabinet to retrieve his files. The entire bullpen watched in silence as he lifted a chaotic stack of loose papers from the cabinet with no clue which documents belonged to which case. As Sparks fumbled to stuff the papers back into the folders, he glanced over his shoulder at the amused stares of his colleagues, who burst into laughter. Feeling like a prisoner walking to the gallows, Sparks made his way to Mullins's office, folders in hand. Mullins took one look at the disorganized mess and instructed Sparks to sit down and close the door behind him.

About two miles away at Osan Airbase, Staff Sergeant Ramirez was hard at work in the pharmacy—not at his job but at harassing the new super attractive Staff Sergeant Isabella Sanchez, who had been stationed at Osan for a few weeks. Isabella, dressed in her blues, had a figure that seemed to defy the limitations of the Air Force's uniform design. Her curves strained against the service-issued nylon pants, and her blouse appeared to be a size too small. As she trained on conducting the medicine inventory, Ramirez repeatedly interrupted with his unwanted advances. "What's up Isabella? When are you gonna give me a chance with all that?" he asked.

Isabella, a seven-year Air Force veteran, wasn't fazed by Ramirez's comments. "I'm gonna give you a chance to walk away from me before I file a sexual harassment complaint," Isabella responded firmly. Isabella knew the best way to deal with Ramirez was to confront him head-on.

About an hour later, Sparks's counseling session ended, and he and Devin drove one of the detachment vehicles to the hospital to visit the pharmacy. As they approached, Devin happened to lock eyes with Isabella, who had moved to the front customer service window. Isabella's gaze lingered as the agents walked toward the side employee entrance. Ramirez, raised around the gang lifestyle by his older brothers in Los Angeles, noticed that Isabella's attention was elsewhere and quickly became irritated.

Devin and Sparks knocked on the side door, and Ramirez, eager to assert himself against any potential competition for Isabella's attention, went to answer it. As soon as he opened the door, he was met with Devin's OSI badge and credentials, just inches from his face.

"Hey, Special Agent Jackson with OSI. I'm here to see Tech Sergeant Wilson."

In an instant, all the cockiness drained from Ramirez's demeanor. His eyes widened in surprise, and he stood speechless. Devin shot a side glance at Sparks to confirm they were both picking up on the same reaction.

"Ah ... oh ... okay, you guys can come on in," Ramirez stammered.

Ramirez stepped to the side to let the agents in and then led them a few feet away to the office of Tech Sergeant Wilson. Ramirez knocked on the door and announced the agents' presence. "Hey, there's two OSI agents here to see you."

Wilson, sitting at his desk, looked at the agents and then turned back to Ramirez, a look of confusion and fear on his face. Sparks shot a quick side-eye to Devin, just to check the vibe.

"Hey, guys, come on in. How can I help you?" Wilson asked, staring at Ramirez as though he'd just been betrayed.

Devin and Sparks took their seats inside Wilson's office as the door was shut behind them. Sparks introduced himself and

Devin, then explained that they were there because of Wilson's inquiry into biological weapons vaccines.

Wilson, still nervous that the agents were there because of his actions, couldn't immediately recall asking for assistance. After a few moments, he remembered the brief conversation he had with Zach over the phone.

The conversation quickly shifted as Wilson brought up his off-base exploits. "You know, things just aren't the same around here anymore."

"What do you mean by that?" Sparks asked.

Wilson, sensing an opportunity to steer the conversation, stretched leisurely and leaned back in his chair as if he were a grandfather about to share an old war story with his grandchildren. "Well, I've been here a long time. This is my third tour in Korea, and back in the day, guys were more respectful. Nowadays, these young guys just don't care. They have no respect for you at all. All they want to do is fight."

"Why would somebody want to fight you?" Devin asked.

Wilson replied, "Because of my girlfriend. She's Ukrainian, and she's beautiful."

"So, guys are rolling up on you, trying to take your woman?" Devin asked.

"Nah, man. She's a juicy girl at one of the bars off-base. These little knuckleheads are always trying to talk to her, and they're getting really disrespectful. One of them tried to fight me the other night," Wilson replied.

Devin and Sparks exchanged a glance of disbelief. Wilson was about fifty pounds overweight, and his posture could be described, at best, as a slouch. But Sparks took the bait.

"Why is your girl causing you so many issues?"

"I'm fine with her being a juicy girl as long as she shows me respect when I'm in the bar. But lately, guys have been propositioning her right in front of me, and many of them get very handsy in the club." Despite his slouchy demeanor, Wilson still had enough pride to confront the G.I.s for disrespecting his girlfriend.

After about half an hour of Wilson's stories about the good old days of dating juicies, he decided to introduce the agents to his boss, Captain Brunelle. The three men walked a few doors down in the pharmacy, and Wilson knocked on Brunelle's door. "Sir, there's two OSI agents here I'd like to introduce to you."

Captain Brunelle, sitting at his desk, was speechless, his eyes widening as he looked at the agents. Finally, he stood up, shook hands, and introduced himself. After another awkward moment, Devin turned to Sparks, who discreetly held up three fingers behind Wilson's back, signifying that all three men in the pharmacy had "freaked out" when introduced to the agents.

Wilson then walked the agents to the door, and they exited through the side entrance.

"So yeah, that was weird," Devin said.

"Yeah, you get used to it after a while, but that was kinda strange," Sparks responded.

Devin laughed. "Do you think his girlfriend is as fine as he says she is?"

"Nah, but he did say she's a juicy girl, so…money goes a long way."

The two agents reached their vehicle, still laughing about their encounter. Sparks, looking forward to his upcoming trip to Busan, decided it was time to make plans.

"It's Friday, man. What's up? We going out?"

"You already know!" Devin replied.

A few hours later, Mr. Viktor Kovalenko, the US State Department's liaison to the United States Forces Korea Headquarters, was sitting in his office when Wilson and Ramirez arrived. "Gentlemen, thank you for coming. Please have a seat. Can I offer you coffee or water, maybe? I'm sorry for disturbing your weekend, but you've been doing a wonderful job, and I wanted to let you know that I've been having some issues with a few of the bar owners. It seems that some of them have been a bit careless. Have you noticed anything alarming? Anything I should be aware of?" Kovalenko asked as the two airmen sat nervously in front of him.

Wilson replied, "No, Mr. Kovalenko, the owners know we mean business when we deal with them."

"Good, good. You know, sometimes I wonder if I should just cut them out of the picture all together. But hey, it is Korea, right? Is there anything else you want to talk to me about?" asked Kovalenko.

Wilson slowly shook his head, but Ramirez saw this as an opportunity to impress Kovalenko.

"Yeah, you know what, we might have some problems coming our way," Ramirez blurted out.

At first, Kovalenko looked annoyed that Ramirez was speaking instead of Wilson, but then he directed Ramirez to continue.

"I think we might have a rat on our team. We got visited by two feds at the pharmacy, and for some reason, they came looking for us just to chit chat."

After that statement, there was no doubt that Ramirez had Kovalenko's full attention.

"Well, what did you tell them?" Kovalenko asked.

"Nothing, we didn't say anything," Ramirez foolishly said as Wilson sat beside him, biting his lip.

"Look, guys, cops don't just knock on your door for no reason. If you've got a rat, it needs to be exterminated. Here's a bit of advice: let this be the last conversation we have about a rat. I trust you to do what is necessary."

With firm instructions from Kovalenko, Wilson and Ramirez left the headquarters building and began plotting their next move.

Later that night, Tori and her friend Kathy arrived at "The Groove," a large nightclub located on a side street about a ten-minute walk from the Osan back gate. Tori had been assigned to Osan a month earlier and worked in the hospital as a medical assistant. Neither she nor Devin knew the other was at Osan, as they had not spoken since Devin left Hawaii for the OSI academy.

The club was packed with people and Tori was dressed conservatively compared to the other young women in the entertainment district. She and Kathy stood along the wall at the rear of the club, watching others dance.

"Tori, girl, you better come on! You've been here for a month, and you're still acting brand new!" Kathy shouted.

"What? No, I'm not. I'm just chill, you know, but I'm still having a good time," Tori said jokingly.

"Well, if you keep turning down all these dudes, eventually they're going to stop trying to talk to you."

Just then, a young man who knew Kathy walked up to deliver a message. "Hey, heads up, the police just got here." Kathy scanned the club for Town Patrol but didn't see any Security Forces troops nearby.

"I don't see the police. Why would they even be in here?" Kathy asked.

As Kathy spoke, Tori looked up and saw Devin and Sparks walking through the club entrance. At first, she couldn't believe it was him, as she had never seen him with a full beard before.

"What's wrong with you?" Kathy asked.

Tori didn't respond; she kept staring at Devin. Suddenly, her feet began to move toward him before she even realized it. Devin and Sparks made their way to the bar to speak to friends who were ordering drinks. Devin felt a tug on his arm and turned around to see who was trying to get his attention. As he turned, he realized the person tugging on him was Ella Mae, who immediately extended her arms to embrace him.

With all of this happening just a few feet in front of her, Tori stopped dead in her tracks. She was too embarrassed to speak to him, so she slowly turned around. As Devin finished his embrace with Ella Mae, he looked up and saw Tori turning away from him. To Devin, it seemed as though Tori had seen him and turned away to avoid speaking to him. He stood there watching Tori walk away until he was pulled to a booth by Ella to join her, Sparks, and Detective Kim.

Devin sat at the booth with his teammates, but all he could think about was Tori. He tried to sneak a few peeks in her direction, but he refused to approach her. Before he could decide what to do, Tori was standing in front of him.

"Hey, can I speak to you for a second?"

Devin excused himself from the booth and walked to the other side of the club with Tori. The two stared at each other nervously until Tori finally broke the ice.

"You're looking good…Special Agent."

"Tori, how long have you been here?"

"I've been on base about a month, but I don't get out too often. How are you enjoying your new job?"

"I love the excitement of the investigations, but the workload is incredibly stressful."

Tori glanced back toward the booth and noticed Ella was staring at her and Devin from across the room.

"You know, I've thought about you a lot since we last spoke, and I'm just really glad to see you're doing well and living out your dreams."

"Thanks," Devin replied. "I guess we get to realize some of our dreams, but not all of them."

"What does that mean?" Tori asked.

"It means it's really good to see you, Tori," Devin whispered in her ear as the music continued to blast. Tori didn't respond immediately but noticed Ella was still staring at her. She grabbed Devin's phone from his hand and put her number in his contacts.

"It looks like you're wanted over there, so here's my number. Give me a call sometime when you're free." Tori walked off to rejoin Kathy as Devin stood there alone, still in disbelief that Tori had re-entered his life. He finally walked back over to the booth with a look of guilt on his face as Ella and Detective Kim gave him the evil eye.

Sparks sensed a different vibe from Devin. "Hey man, who was that?"

Devin, knowing Ella would be hanging on every word, nervously replied, "That's Tori, someone I used to know, back in the day."

Sparks could tell that Devin was acting a bit strangely, but he was more concerned by the way Ella seemed to be squirming in her seat, staring at Tori as she made her way back across the crowd to meet Kathy.

Sparks chuckled. "What the hell's wrong with you?"

Detective Kim quickly looked away to avoid embarrassing Ella any further.

"Nothing," Ella replied. She tried to look down at her phone but couldn't help but glance at Devin's face, trying to read his expression. Although the four of them were just hanging out as friends, Ella was secretly hoping that she and Devin could have a moment together at some point during the night. That had been the plan before Tori decided to show up. Devin, sensing the tension, attempted to change the subject by asking Detective Kim what she was drinking.

As Detective Kim was responding, Sparks tapped Devin on the arm. "Hey man, we gotta go!"

Devin didn't know what had caused Sparks to react that way, but he trusted his instincts. The two agents grabbed the girls by their hands and pulled them toward the exit. As they neared the door, Devin remembered Tori was still inside with her friend. He motioned for Ella to exit with Sparks as he turned back to find Tori. He finally spotted her and managed to make eye contact through the crowd. He motioned for her to come with him. Tori wasn't sure why Devin was signaling her to leave, but she didn't want to abandon Kathy, and she definitely didn't want any drama with his staring female friend. So, she motioned for Devin to go ahead without her.

Devin turned and joined Sparks, Ella, and Detective Kim, who were standing outside a café across the street from the club.

"What's going on? What did you see?" Devin asked Sparks.

"Man, those cats from two weeks ago who were fighting the Army dudes at the NCO club just walked in. Those Army guys were already in the club, and I saw them recognize each other. I wasn't trying to get these girls caught up in some stupid shit!"

"Yeah, you're right," Devin agreed.

Ella and Detective Kim were still unsure why they had to leave so abruptly. Suddenly, they heard loud screams coming from the club as people began to run out. A few seconds later, several Town Patrol officers sprinted toward the establishment. The crowd poured out of the exit as a massive fight broke out inside the club. Several people were getting trampled, as the club only had one exit to accommodate the approximately three hundred patrons to leave. As people fled the building, Devin began to worry about Tori. Suddenly, she appeared, hobbling out of the club wearing one shoe, while Kathy's shirt was drenched in someone's expensive drink.

Ella saw Tori limping through the crowd and began to laugh. "I could have sworn she had two shoes on earlier."

Devin tried to make his way over to Tori, but she waved him off and continued to hobble toward the taxi line to catch a ride back to the airbase. Devin and Sparks waited outside the club to get a briefing from Town Patrol before heading home.

Later that night, in a much more low-key establishment not too far away, the crew from the pharmacy—Wilson, Ramirez, and Brunelle—were shooting pool and drinking at a bar. Wilson and Ramirez took turns buying shots, and by this point, Brunelle was extremely intoxicated. Eventually, Brunelle was so inebriated that he couldn't stand on his own without holding on to the wall. Wilson saw that the time was right and suggested Brunelle call it a night.

"Captain, I think you're good, bro. You should probably head out."

"Yeah, yeah, I'm kinda tired," Brunelle responded. Wilson gave a slight nod to Ramirez to carry out the plan.

"Come on, man, I'll help you catch a cab," said Ramirez as he helped Brunelle stumble down the steps to the street.

Ramirez dragged Brunelle down to an alley connected to a dimly lit side road. Brunelle continued to stumble as they walked. Once Ramirez felt confident that they were isolated, he began his interrogation.

"Alright, so tell me the truth, man. Did they flip you? Are they coming for us?"

Brunelle, who could hardly focus his eyes on Ramirez, stared back in confusion. "Who? What are you talking about? Who's coming for us?"

"OSI! Is OSI coming? Did they get to you?" Ramirez yelled.

Still confused, Brunelle responded, "Man, I don't know what you're talking about. I just need to go home."

"You don't know? Oh, okay, so they just showed up to the office for no reason, huh? Dang, my bad, I'm tripping, man. That's my fault," Ramirez muttered, trying to calm Brunelle down.

Brunelle believed Ramirez's apology was sincere and started to let his guard down. He relieved himself while standing against the alley wall. While Brunelle wasn't looking, Ramirez reached behind a dumpster and retrieved an item he had planted there a few hours earlier. Brunelle turned around to light a cigarette, and suddenly Ramirez struck him on the right side of his head with the blunt object. Brunelle fell to the ground, but Ramirez continued to hit him in the face. Brunelle cried out for Ramirez to stop, but the beating continued. Ramirez seemed intent on ending Brunelle's life right there in the alley until he saw the headlights of a taxi approaching. Ramirez managed to get the semi-conscious Brunelle to his feet, flagging down the taxi, and pushed Brunelle into the back seat.

"Hey man, he's a bit drunk. Just drop him off at his house, and he'll be alright. He can sleep it off," Ramirez told the taxi driver as he gave him Brunelle's address and handed him twenty dollars for the ride.

The taxi driver took a quick peek into the back seat, saw Brunelle slumped over, and assumed Ramirez was telling the truth. The driver then pulled away with Brunelle in the back seat, close to death.

A few minutes later, the taxi arrived at Brunelle's apartment. Believing that Brunelle had passed out in the back seat, the cab driver yelled at him to wake up and exit the vehicle. Brunelle came to, stepped out of the cab, and fell to the ground. The taxi driver began to drive away but noticed Brunelle lying on the sidewalk. He pulled out his cell phone and called the Osan Law Enforcement Desk. "Hey, this is Wu. I drive taxis in Songtan. I got a drunk GI on the sidewalk—well, I think he's drunk. You should send somebody to come get him."

A few minutes later, two Security Forces Town Patrol airmen arrived at Brunelle's apartment to find him lying in a pool of blood. They turned him over to check if he was breathing and noticed he had been severely beaten. Brunelle's right eye was hanging out of its socket, and he had several contusions on his head. The Town Patrol called for an ambulance to take him to the trauma center in Seoul.

The day after the assault, Agent Sparks arrived at his hotel in Busan. While waiting in line to check in, he noticed a beautiful European woman working behind the desk. She finished with the customer in front of him and called Sparks forward.

"Hello, sir. Welcome to the Busan Intercontinental Hotel. How may I help you?"

"Good afternoon. I'm just checking in. Last name is Sparks, Alexander," he replied.

"Okay, Mr. Sparks, I have you with us for three nights. Is that correct?" the woman asked.

Trying not to show how enamored he was with the woman, Sparks nodded and tried to avoid making too much eye contact with her.

"Okay, great. And what brings you to Busan, if you don't mind me asking?"

Sparks paused for a second to ensure his response didn't sound rehearsed. "I'm just in town to help out a friend for a couple of days."

The woman smiled. "Oh, that's nice of you. I'll just need to see your passport."

Sparks handed her the document. She walked away from the front desk to make a photocopy, then returned and handed it back to Sparks.

"Here's your room key and Wi-Fi password. The restaurant is open until nine, and the bar is open until eleven. You should stop by; the bartender is good."

Sparks took his passport from her and noticed she wasn't wearing a wedding ring. "Okay, thanks. I just might stop by a little later tonight. What was your name again?"

"Sophia," the woman replied, flashing a seductive smile at Sparks, who then turned and walked toward the hotel elevator.

Devin and Zachary visited the trauma center in Seoul later that day, after being assigned the attempted murder case. When they arrived, they found Captain Brunelle in an induced coma with a large bandage covering the right side of his face. The agents read his charts and pulled a nurse aside to inquire about the seriousness of Brunelle's injuries. The nurse explained that Brunelle had nearly asphyxiated in the ambulance after choking on his own vomit. Surgeons had to remove his right eye, and he was placed him in a coma to allow his body to heal from the trauma to his skull. There was no estimate of how long he would remain in the coma or if he would ever fully recover.

Although he had no evidence at the time, Devin couldn't help but wonder if his and Sparks's visit to the pharmacy had anything to do with Brunelle being beaten within an inch of his life. "Zach, I don't know if I'm trippin' or not, but what are the odds of me and Al dropping by the pharmacy, and later that night, this guy almost gets beaten to death? I don't know if they were involved with this at all, but I do know they acted really weird when we showed our credentials."

Zach nodded in agreement. "Yeah, that does seem a bit strange. Well, there's only one way to know. Let's ask them."

They returned to Osan later that night, and Devin decided to drive over to the base Shoppette to buy a gallon of milk. The Shoppette was like the neighborhood corner store—most people went there only to buy a couple of things, just enough to hold them over until they had time to go to the larger commissary. As Devin was walking back to the beverage freezer, he noticed an older Korean woman pushing two large shopping carts loaded to capacity with products. Upon taking a second look, he noticed the woman had several packs of each item.

Why does this woman have five packs of cheese and four packs of bologna? he wondered. Then it hit him—this is what Agent Mullins had asked him to investigate: black marketing. The woman was looking around the store nervously and spotted Devin staring at her as she pushed her carts up to the cashier. Devin quickly found the store manager, covertly showed his badge, and told the manager that he needed a copy of the woman's receipt after she paid for the items. The manager agreed, but when Devin turned around, the woman was nowhere to be found. He ran outside to the parking lot and saw no trace of her. Just as he was about to leave, he heard a loud rattling sound.

He looked up and saw the woman, now pushing a cart full of products, exiting the back door of the Shoppette and running full speed toward the taxi line. Devin couldn't help but laugh as she darted across the parking lot. He began to jog over to the taxi line, but the taxi driver jumped out of his car and helped her throw the items into the trunk.

"Wait, stop!" Devin yelled, but the taxi sped out of the parking lot. Still amused by the woman's athletic ability, Devin walked over to the next taxi, showed the driver his badge, and asked where the other taxi was headed. The driver looked at him, shrugged, and said, "What's going on, black marketing?"

"What? Why would you say that?" Devin responded. At that moment, he realized just how expansive this investigation could get.

The next day, Zach and Devin coordinated with Capt. Murphy from the JAG office regarding Wilson and Ramirez and were met with a surprise response. "I know him. We went to high school together, and he was best friends with my high school boyfriend." The agents expected Capt. Murphy to immediately recuse herself from the investigation, but she felt confident that her past acquaintances wouldn't interfere with her work.

Later that day, Wilson and Ramirez were both escorted to the detachment by their First Sergeant and interviewed separately. First up was Agent Zachary and Detective Kim, who conducted an interview with Ramirez. After a few minutes of rapport building, Zach began asking direct questions regarding Ramirez's whereabouts on the night of the assault. Ramirez seemed well-prepared for the interview and never wavered in his story.

"We were all hanging out that night. Me, Brunelle, and Wilson were at a bar that we always go to, shooting pool. Brunelle had too much to drink and started stumbling and falling over the table. I hated seeing him like that, you know, especially since he's an officer, so I helped him down the stairs and walked him over to the taxi line. When the taxi showed up, I gave him Brunelle's address and a few dollars to cover the fare. That was the last time I saw Brunelle. He was fine when I put him in the taxi. What do you guys think happened to him?"

Although Ramirez's story was plausible, his cocky demeanor didn't sit well with Zach, who felt that Ramirez had been less than truthful.

In the other interview room, Devin and Mullins began questioning Wilson, whose behavior was identical to when the agents had visited his office. He wouldn't stop talking, but instead of speaking about the incident, he kept trying to change the subject back to bar girls and the "good ol' days" at Osan. Devin pressed Wilson to stay focused on the line of questioning. Wilson's story was remarkably similar to Ramirez's. He claimed their crew was drinking at a Korean bar, and Ramirez walked Brunelle down to the taxi line. According to Wilson, Ramirez returned to the bar after about fifteen minutes, and he didn't notice him acting strangely.

Wilson didn't exhibit the same self-absorbed demeanor as Ramirez, but he was very eager to know what evidence the agents had already collected and who they thought might have assaulted Brunelle. At one point, Wilson's questions became a little too personal.

"Hey, Jackson, do you guys have a confidential informant working on the investigation?" Wilson asked.

Devin looked up from his notes and didn't immediately respond. He wondered why Wilson would even ask such a question. "No, we don't have any informants," Devin said, shaking his head in frustration from not getting useful information during the interview.

When the interviews were complete, Wilson and Ramirez were released back to the First Sergeant, who drove them back to work at the pharmacy. By this time, all the other workers had completed their assignments and left for the day. Being alone in the office, Wilson finally began to show his true emotions about being interviewed by the agents.

"Hey man, I trust you stuck to the plan and didn't say anything. You know you can count on me, right? But look, things are getting too hot around here. We may need to cut back on the pills until things cool down a bit."

Ramirez, who was looking for a way to get Wilson out of the picture, agreed—only to keep Wilson in the dark about his true intentions: to replace him.

CHAPTER 4
THE CONNECT

Ramirez, feeling confident about his performance with OSI the previous day, made his way down the main street in Songtan. He turned down a side road and walked through a narrow alleyway. He stopped and knocked on a door, which was opened by a sixty-year-old Korean man who recognized Ramirez and let him inside the building.

"You're late. Where's Wilson?" the man asked.

"Mr. So, don't worry about Wilson. He ain't gonna be around for a while. Look, no load today. OSI was snooping around, and…Wilson got a bit spooked," said Ramirez.

Mr. So was confused and demanded that Ramirez hand over the pills he had agreed to buy. "I'm trying to tell you we gotta chill on the pills for a few days, bro. I ain't trying to get caught up over some stupid oxycodone!" Ramirez yelled.

Mr. So was not pleased to learn that he couldn't meet the demand. "My customers need the pills. Wilson told me there was no problem. Now you tell me there's a problem. Where's Wilson? My boss is not going to be happy!"

Ramirez saw an opening to demean Mr. So. "I thought you were the boss."

Mr. So recognized Ramirez's sarcasm and quickly responded, "I own the bar, but I'm not the boss. Got it?"

"Well, look, don't worry about Wilson. I got you. When things cool off, I'll be back with the stuff."

Ramirez exited the building and walked back through the alley to the main road. Standing about twenty yards away was a group of young Koreans, smoking and hanging out near their motorcycles. Unbeknownst to Ramirez, one of the cyclists happened to be Detective Kim, who overheard bits of Ramirez's conversation with Mr. So. She tried not to show too much concern toward Ramirez, as she was working undercover on a motorcycle theft investigation for the KNP.

After leaving the bar owner in Songtan, Ramirez decided to catch the train to Seoul and pay a surprise visit to Kovalenko at his office inside USFK. He wasn't sure how Kovalenko would react to his visit, but he needed to find a way to push Wilson out of the top spot so that he could report directly to Kovalenko. Ramirez arrived at USFK and used his military ID to enter the building. Once inside, he asked for directions to Kovalenko's office and introduced himself to Kovalenko's secretary, who then called to alert him of Ramirez's visit. The secretary gave Ramirez permission to enter Kovalenko's office, and he proceeded with his annoying cockiness on full display.

"Shut the door! What the hell are you doing here?" Kovalenko shouted.

"Hey, Mr. Kovalenko, I just wanted to stop by and give you some good news," Ramirez replied.

Kovalenko, a savvy individual, could instantly see through Ramirez's fake charm. He knew Ramirez was only there because something bad had happened or they were on the verge of a small catastrophe. Ramirez walked around Kovalenko's office, looking at pictures of his daughters.

"Look, I just wanted to let you know that I took care of my rodent problem. It shouldn't be an issue going forward," Ramirez said with a nervous laugh, unsure of how Kovalenko would respond.

Kovalenko, still uneasy about Ramirez's presence, questioned his true intentions. "Why am I hearing this from you and not Wilson?"

Ramirez saw an opening to strike and took it. "See, that's the thing, man. You know, I was thinking about what you said last time about cutting the bar owner out. Well, I think you were right. We should. And we should also cut Wilson out. I could work directly for you," Ramirez proclaimed.

Kovalenko was relieved that Ramirez didn't want to discuss something more serious, but he didn't show any emotion, wanting to keep Ramirez on his toes. Kovalenko slowly sat back down in his chair and began to question Ramirez.

"I think you need to think about what you're saying. People don't just…walk away from this much money. So why don't you take your dumb ass out of here and don't come back. Because I don't think you're ready to do what you're insinuating."

Initially, Ramirez was not happy with Kovalenko's response, but then he realized that Kovalenko was giving him an opportunity to prove himself. He flashed a guilty smile toward Kovalenko as he made his way to the door. "I guess we'll see, Papi."

"Stop!" Kovalenko called out, sensing that Ramirez was willing to do the demanding work to gain his approval. He wanted to make sure Ramirez understood exactly what he was getting himself into.

"How much do you really know about our arrangement?" Kovalenko asked.

Showing his ignorance, Ramirez blurted out the first thing that came to his mind. "I know there's a lot of money in getting these girls to sell their asses. The game is easy: the girls get the guys drunk in the bars, sit on their laps, and talk dirty to them. Then Ajeema comes over and tells the guys they can take the girls home for a hundred dollars. They offer some cheap Viagra to go with it. Once they get to the hotel, the girls sell them the dope, and we all get paid."

Kovalenko wasn't surprised by Ramirez's response. It had been his intention to keep Ramirez and Wilson in the dark about his true operations. "Ramirez, your ignorance is astonishing. However, you may be better served by your mental incapacities. If I were you, I'd accept things as you know them."

"Hold on, man," Ramirez replied. "What are you saying? I'm bringing in a lot of money for you guys, and now you're insulting my intelligence? Whatever's going on, I want in. Alright?"

Kovalenko stood up and walked over to Ramirez, fixing him with a steely gaze. "Are you sure? Are you ready to betray your country?"

Ramirez was thoroughly confused. "Betray my country? Over some hookers? What's really going on, Mr. Kovalenko?"

Kovalenko turned away, picking up a picture of himself with his two daughters. "Every time I walk into one of those bars and see those 'juicy girls,' I feel disgusted. You'd think after all these years we'd have a better method of intelligence collection, but the world's oldest profession remains the most effective."

Ramirez was completely lost. "Yeah, I don't get it."

"As I expected. You see, I was raised in Ukraine. Most of my family still lives there. Over the past several years, the US has provided billions in aid to support our efforts against the Russian Federation. However, we always knew that one day, that aid would stop. Then what? Look at what happened in Afghanistan and Iraq when America pulled out. So we decided to study how the US military operates in a cold-war environment—when the enemy is merely a few kilometers away, and you know they could strike at any moment. And what better place to study that than Korea, where the war has been on pause for the last seventy-five years."

Ramirez stood speechless, trying to process what Kovalenko was saying. He thought he was dealing with a simple prostitution ring and had no idea it was connected to Ukraine. "Wait a minute, but you work for the American government."

Kovalenko was quick to correct him. "No, I work at the American government. I work for the Ukrainian people. This was never about prostitution, trafficking, or even the drugs. We use the girls to get the G.I.s drunk and high, and then they gather military intelligence and bring it back to us. We have agents all over South Korea, not just in the bars. Trafficking is a necessary evil, one I regret, but I must do what's in the best interest of my people. And if I didn't do it, someone else would."

Ramirez stood there, trying to grasp the full scope of what Kovalenko had just revealed. Kovalenko had successfully achieved the shock he intended. "I tried to tell you to walk away, but now you know the truth. So, you have a decision to make."

Ramirez slowly backed up to the office door, staring at the floor before raising his eyes to meet Kovalenko's. "Alright, I'm in."

Four hours away in Busan, Agent Sparks exited the elevator into the hotel lobby. With no work scheduled until the next day, he strolled over to the hotel bar and grabbed a drink menu. Before he could catch the bartender's attention, he felt a tap on his shoulder—it was Sophia, still wearing her name tag from the front desk.

"Hi, Mr. Sparks, I see you decided to try our magnificent bar."

Sparks turned, surprised that Sophia had walked up behind him undetected. "Oh hey, yeah, I was a bit bored, so I came down for a quick drink. Would you like to join me?" he asked.

Sophia agreed, and the two moved to a more secluded area of the bar. Over the next hour, their table became increasingly crowded with empty glasses. Realizing he had probably had too much to drink, Sparks decided to call it a night.

"I apologize, but I'm going to have to cut this short. I've got to get up early for work tomorrow."

"Sure, I understand," Sophia replied as she began to search her purse for her car keys. Once she found them, she stood up and pretended to be a little wobbly to gain Sparks's sympathy.

Sparks noticed her unsteadiness and offered to walk her outside to catch a cab, but Sophia had no intention of leaving that night. "No, please don't! I don't want the other front desk workers to see me like this. Can I just come to your room and take a quick nap on the couch? All I need is an hour, and I promise I'll be out of your way."

Sparks was genuinely concerned for Sophia's welfare, but he didn't want her to know who he really was or what he was doing in Busan. However, he reluctantly agreed to let Sophia come up to his room.

The two left the bar and made their way to the elevator. Sparks swiped his room card across the reader and pushed the button for the twelfth floor. As soon as the doors closed, Sophia became extremely flirtatious, suddenly forgetting how to stand on her own and needing to press her body against his. They made their way to his room, where Sophia immediately kicked off her shoes and lay down on the couch.

Surprised that she didn't try to make her way to the bedroom, Sparks retrieved an extra blanket from the closet and laid it across Sophia's body. He went to use the restroom and found Sophia asleep when he returned. He walked over to the dresser, placed his wallet, badge, and credentials inside the top drawer, and then laid down in the bed. He grabbed the remote to turn off the television, which plunged the suite into darkness. Before he could settle his mind for the night, he felt the bed shake. He opened his eyes to nothing but darkness and the warmth of Sophia's body sliding closer to him. Sparks was paralyzed, unsure how to change the situation without blowing his cover. He decided to do nothing and let Sophia dictate the situation.

The next morning, Sophia woke up and eased her way out of bed without waking Sparks. She picked her dress up from the floor and quickly threw it over her head. She grabbed her keys from the dresser and noticed the top drawer slightly open. Sophia turned around to confirm that Sparks was still sleeping. She cautiously opened the drawer and saw Sparks's belongings. She opened his wallet and saw his OSI badge and credentials. Just then, Sparks stirred, causing Sophia to quickly close the drawer and hurriedly say goodbye as she rushed out of the room.

Sparks felt uneasy about Sophia's quick departure and immediately jumped up to check the security of his property. He noticed the drawer was not fully closed and his badge was facing upward; at that moment, he knew without a doubt that Sophia was aware of his true identity.

Sophia exited the elevator and quickly walked past the front desk to leave the hotel. She reached her vehicle and sat there for a moment, trying to process what she had just discovered. Sophia pulled her cell phone from her purse and made a call to her father, Viktor Kovalenko.

"Hey, it's me. Yeah, I'm just wrapping up." She reached back into her purse and pulled out a copy of Sparks's passport that she made when he checked into the hotel. "I wasn't sure, but your hunch was correct. He's one of them!"

The next morning, Devin and Zachary sat at their desks, working on their individual case files. Detective Kim was on a phone call in the front office at Ella's desk. After she hung up, she walked back to Devin and Zachary with a very confused look on her face.

"I don't know which one of you should handle this, but the First Sergeant from Civil Engineering is about to bring one of his troops over here."

"For what?" Zachary asked.

Detective Kim replied, "I'm not sure. Something about how he got married and wasn't supposed to or something like that."

Zachary was the duty agent for the week and would normally take all the walk-in reports, but he was up to his chest in paperwork. He looked over to Devin to ask for an assist. "DJ, man, I can't take this one. I've got to finish prepping for this sexual assault interview."

"Alright, I got it," Devin responded.

Ten minutes later, Airman Franklin was sitting in the interrogation room. Before beginning the interview, Devin spoke to Franklin's First Sergeant, who informed him that he had warned Franklin about marrying "that strange woman" and had given him direct orders not to go to the Ukrainian Embassy.

Unfortunately, Airman Franklin was in love with the first girl who had ever paid him any attention, and he valued her instructions more than his chain of command or his career.

After the briefing, Devin stepped into the interview room, accompanied by Detective Kim, who sat quietly taking notes. Devin began the interview by asking routine background questions and quickly noticed that the airman was terrified. Franklin only gave one- or two-word responses to Devin's questions, and his voice was so low that the agents could barely hear him from just a few feet away. Franklin explained that Osan was his first assignment, and he had only been on station for five months.

Not fully understanding why Franklin's unit had a problem with his marriage, Devin came right out and asked why there was so much tension between Franklin and his leadership.

"I wasn't going to do it. My shirt and my commander told me not to, but she kept pushing," Franklin said.

Devin looked over t Detective Kim, who returned the same confused look he was giving her. "Your wife, is she a Korean woman?" Devin asked.

"No, she's Ukrainian," Franklin responded.

Devin sat there, wondering how a bumbling idiot like Airman Franklin had managed to marry a Ukrainian woman in South Korea.

"Hold up…is she a juicy girl?" Devin asked.

Franklin nodded in embarrassment. "Yeah, she was. She quit when we got married." Devin was still confused about the situation and prodded the airman to tell him the entire story.

"About a month after we met, she said she loved me, and she pressured me to marry her. As soon as we got married, she started begging me to sponsor her brother to come into the country. So, I filled out a bunch of documents and sent my passport and birth certificate to the Ukrainian Embassy. About a month later, the brother showed up, but I haven't seen him since the day he arrived. And now she's starting to disappear for days at a time."

Devin and Detective Kim sat in disbelief as they listened to the airman's story. Franklin sat there with his head down, afraid that he had ruined his military career less than a year after it began.

"Airman Franklin, do you understand what's really going on?" Devin asked.

Franklin continued staring at the floor and made eye contact just long enough to shake his head.

"Yeah, I figured you didn't," Devin said as he leaned back in his chair and grabbed a counterintelligence pamphlet off the table. "So, basically, what has happened is that you've been the victim of a honeypot. You got seduced by a pretty girl who's probably way out of your league, and she used you not only for money but also for benefits now that you're married. She's been pumping you for information about your job, military exercises, and deployments, and worst of all, you provided your documents to bring her 'brother' into the country. You do know that dude's not her real brother, right? And now you don't know the location of either one of them. Is it starting to sink in yet? Do you understand just how bad you f'd up?"

Airman Franklin began to panic and nervously looked around the room for an exit, but he didn't make it. After emitting a strange noise from his throat, he vomited and caught it in his mouth. Devin was disgusted but didn't want to embarrass the airman any further.

"Do you need to use the restroom?" Devin asked.

Franklin nodded while holding his right hand over his mouth to prevent any spillage onto the floor. When Franklin returned from the restroom, he was released back to his First Sergeant.

Devin walked back to the bullpen, shaking his head at yet another situation that seemed too ridiculous to believe. As he entered, he was greeted by Ella Mae, who had apparently watched the entire interview from the monitor in the bullpen.

"What kind of fool sends his passport and birth certificate to the Ukrainian Embassy?" she asked.

"That's a good question," Devin replied. "I want to believe he's just young and naïve instead of a spy, but I guess we'll have to see how this plays out."

Later that afternoon, Devin assisted Zach with the subject interview for his sexual assault case. Zach took the lead in the interview while Devin sat at the desk and took notes.

"So, help me understand. Was she drunk or not?" Zach asked the Staff Sergeant, who continued to slump over in his seat, refusing to make eye contact with the agents.

"Well, yeah, she was drunk, but she knew who I was," he replied.

Feeling the need to press harder, Zach asked, "How do you know she recognized you?"

Believing he was about to share information that would exonerate him, the Staff Sergeant raised his head and boldly proclaimed, "Because when I pushed my way into her dorm room, she said, 'Hey, Rodney, what are you doing kicking my door in?'"

The two agents exchanged looks of confusion and tried not to laugh, realizing that Rodney had basically confessed to breaking into the victim's dorm room.

Suddenly, Ella Mae knocked on the door to the interrogation room. Devin cracked the door open to see Ella waving at the agents to step out into the hallway. Zachary paused the interview, and he and Devin exited to the hallway to see what had Ella so excited.

"Hey, I don't know if this is important or not, but I was looking through his stuff, and I noticed this little bag hanging out of his wallet," Ella whispered.

Zach wasn't very happy with Ella's actions and asked, "Why were you in his wallet in the first place?"

"That's a good question, but that's the wrong question. The right question is, what are these pills in this bag?"

Devin took the bag from Ella and held it up to inspect the pills. "I can't tell what they are, but it looks like it's been stamped by the base pharmacy. The only way to know for sure is to ask your guy."

Zach agreed, and the two agents returned to the interview. As Zach slowly sat back down in his chair, he lifted the plastic bag up and shook it directly in Rodney's face.

"Look, man, you're already in a world of trouble. So, I'm going to give you one chance to answer the question. What's in this bag?"

Rodney hesitated at first, but then seemed relieved to be talking about anything other than the sexual assault. "It's oxy and Viagra."

Zach's face became stern as he wondered why Rodney gave up the information so easily. "You wouldn't happen to have a prescription for oxycodone, would you?"

Rodney shook his head. "No, I don't have a prescription. I got it at the club."

Devin followed up by asking which club he was referring to.

"Any club. If there's juicies there, they got oxy."

"That doesn't make sense," Devin said. "So, what, they're just handing it out?"

Rodney laughed at Devin's question. "Nah, you gotta buy it. But it's cheap, real cheap. As soon as you show interest in one of the girls, the bar owners show up with the pills."

After another hour of interviewing, Zach felt confident that he had enough information for his sexual assault case, and they released Rodney back to his First Sergeant. Devin and Zachary headed back to the bullpen and joined Ella and Detective Kim. Zach placed the bag of pills on Devin's desk.

"So, do you think we need to worry about those pills?"

Before Devin could respond, Detective Kim interrupted. "Hey Devin, who's that guy you spoke to a few days ago at the pharmacy?"

"Tech Sergeant Wilson. Why, what's up?"

"Nah, not him. The Latino guy."

"Oh, you mean Staff Sergeant Ramirez."

"Yeah, that's him. It may be nothing, but you might want to make sure he's on the up and up," Kim suggested.

Devin was still in the dark about what had made Kim suspicious, but he knew there must be something going on for her to intervene in on-base issues. "Cool, thanks, Kim. I'll make a call."

As Devin searched through his list of contacts at the Medical Group, Zach walked out of the bullpen toward the restroom, leaving Devin, Ella, and Detective Kim in the office. Sensing that the vibe was too intense, Ella leaned over and whispered to Devin, but Detective Kim overheard the conversation.

"Hey, you still got that Viagra?" Ella asked.

"Nah, I logged it into evidence after the interview."

Ella gave Devin a look as though he were sitting in the corner wearing a dunce hat. "So that's what y'all be doing? Y'all just be wasting … you know what, never mind!" Ella said jokingly, and she pushed the back of Devin's head down while walking back to her desk in the front office.

Detective Kim laughed as Devin remained impervious to Ella's playful advances.

CHAPTER 5
JUICY

After work was done for the day; Devin, Zach, and Detective Kim went to dinner at a bar in the entertainment district. As the group laughed about the bizarreness of some of their cases, Devin posed a serious question to Zach. "Have you ever noticed that none of these juicy girls are Korean? They're mostly Filipina."

Zach thought for a second. "Yeah, now that you mention it, I guess I never really paid too much attention to it."

Devin nodded. "Yeah, it took a while for me to notice it, too. Kim, how long has it been like this?"

Detective Kim, with her face buried in a plate of chicken wings, looked up and seemed happy that someone had finally asked her opinion. "I've only been in this province for two years, but it's been like this the whole time. Outside of here, and the districts near the other US bases, it's practically non-existent," said Kim.

"So basically, they're here because we're here. Is that what you're saying?" Devin asked.

"That's exactly what I'm saying."

The mood at the table quickly changed to self-reflection upon the realization that the airbase's existence created a hub for human trafficking. Feeling the need to lighten the conversation, Zach leaned over to Devin. "Hey man, can I ask you a serious question?"

"Of course."

"What kind of underwear do you have on?"

Devin slowly turned toward Zach with a look of disgust.

"Hold on, man!" Zach exclaimed. "The other day, Ella asked me if I wore boxers or briefs. I've always worn briefs. Am I missing something? What's up with boxers?"

Devin was still confused by the question but quickly realized that Ella had been up to her shenanigans again. "Boxers, man, I wear boxers. They give you more freedom."

"What kind of freedom?"

Devin was worried that someone else might overhear their conversation. "Dude! You just gotta try them!"

"Seriously? Okay. I thought Ella was just messing with me."

"Look, if I were you, I'd do whatever she says. She knows what she's talking about."

"Wow, okay, she's told me a bunch of other stuff. I just brushed her off. I think I'll start paying more attention to her."

Detective Kim finished eating her wings while holding back her laughter. "Okay, I've heard enough about your underwear for one day. Let's get out of here!"

As they stood up from their table, Zach spotted a juicy girl sitting on the lap of an older, drunken Korean man. The girl was crying and trying to hide the shame on her face. Zach took a few steps toward the girl and asked if she was alright.

"Yes, I'm sorry, I'm sorry," the girl replied.

The girl appeared to be in her early twenties and was dressed in a cheerleader's uniform, with long tube socks and cheap sneakers. Zach told the girl she did not have to apologize and asked her why she was crying.

The old Korean man did not appreciate Zach interfering with his date. "She's fine. I paid for her. Go away!" the man yelled.

Detective Kim, standing by the exit, saw the man's reaction. She purposely let out a sizable yawn and stretch that revealed her gun to the drunk man. The man saw that Detective Kim was packing and quickly decided he didn't want any drama, so he pushed the juicy girl off his lap, grabbed his hat, and made his way out of the establishment.

Once the man left, Zach again asked the girl if she was alright.

"Yeah, I'm just homesick, that's all."

"I'll tell you what, since there's nobody else here, we'll hang out with you for a little bit," Zach said to the girl as he motioned for his friends to come back inside the bar.

The girl became frightened and backed away from Zach. "I'm sorry. I can't sit with customers unless they buy drinks from the bar. Boss will get mad."

Devin realized this might be a good opportunity to gain experience about the inner workings of the juicy bars, so he offered to order a couple of drinks to keep the girl's attention and to keep the bar owner away from their conversation.

The girl signaled the bartender to bring four drinks to the table, and then she introduced herself as "Samantha." Once the drinks arrived, Samantha appeared to revert to her training and began to ask probing questions.

"Thank you very much for the drink. Were you guys looking for company tonight?"

Zachary replied, "No, we just saw you were upset, and I wanted to check on you. So, what makes a pretty girl like you so sad?"

Samantha paused as she looked around to make sure no one was listening to her conversation. "I'm just ready to go home, back to the Philippines."

Devin had a confused look on his face. "Well, why don't you just go home?"

"I can't," replied Samantha. "The boss won't let me leave."

Detective Kim nodded as if she already knew what was going on. Devin needed more answers. "What do you mean he won't let you leave? And who is this boss you're talking about?"

With that question, Samantha began to shut down a bit. "I'm sorry, I'm not supposed to say. Too many people in here. Boss man will know!"

Just then, an older Korean woman approached the table. "She's a pretty girl. You like? She's pretty; you take her home tonight?" the woman asked Zach.

Samantha intervened and explained that they were just having a drink and talking.

"Well, hang on a second. How much to take her home?" Zach asked the woman, who began to grope Samantha to highlight her breasts to Zach.

"For you, $150."

Zach glanced over at Devin to see if he approved of the expense. Devin pulled a wad of cash out of his pants pocket and slid the money over to the woman, who snatched it with no hesitation. The cash was his contingency funds he had signed out from the detachment about two weeks prior.

"What about you? You want a girl too?"

Devin shook his head.

"Okay, you go outside, and she'll be there in five minutes," said the woman as she pulled Samantha from the table.

Devin, Zach, and Detective Kim walked toward the exit, but they were stopped by the Korean bar owner. The owner asked if it was their first time visiting his establishment. Zach confirmed that it was his first time there.

"Oh, okay. I see you have a pretty girl tonight. She'll give you lots of fun!"

"Yeah, maybe," Zach answered.

"Hey, since it's your first time, I have something for you. It's free. Next time you pay," the man said as he handed a small bag to Zach and walked away.

Zach took the bag and then joined Devin and Detective Kim in the alleyway.

"What did that dude give you, a coupon?" Devin asked.

Zach held the bag up to the light to examine its contents. "Nah, he gave me two oxy pills."

At the sound of a door slamming, the agents looked up and saw that Samantha had made her way into the alley through the club's back door. Although she was happy to be out of the club, she had a look of concern on her face because she didn't know what Zach had in store for her.

"Are we going back to your place?" she asked nervously.

Zach was a bit embarrassed by the question and quickly made his intentions known. "No, we just wanted to talk to you. You seemed a bit shaken in the bar."

Relieved by Zach's answer, Samantha nodded. "Yes, the boss can be a very mean man. I didn't want him to get mad at me and add more time."

No one seemed to understand exactly what Samantha meant. "Add time to what?" Devin asked.

Before answering the question, Samantha peeked down the alleyway to make sure they were alone. "We all signed contracts with the bar owners to come here and sing for the GIs. When we got here, they took our passports and made us work in the bars."

Still confused by the explanation, Zach asked Samantha why she didn't just leave and go back to the Philippines. Samantha described how she only got two hours a day to leave the club with the other girls. When she was not working in the bar as a juicy girl or helping to clean up, she would be locked in a cage beside the other Filipinas. The bar owners took their passports from them as soon as they got into South Korea, so leaving the country was not an option.

"Hold up!" Devin interrupted. "Did you say you sleep in a cage?"

"Yes, but don't say anything," Samantha replied. "And ... they make us prostitute to earn money. If we make enough, we can buy our passports back from the owner and go home before the year contract has expired."

As Samantha was talking, Devin noticed two older Korean men standing in the alley, seemingly interested in their conversation. "Heads up, I think we need to go," Devin said.

Having seen the same two men, Zach agreed. "Yeah, I think you're right. Samantha, we'll be back in a couple of days to check in on you. Here's my card. If you ever need anything, just give it to one of the Town Patrol." Zach handed his business card to Samantha, and the agents left her alone in the alley as they made their way back to the airbase.

The following day, Devin, Zach, and Ella were working inside the detachment. As lunch approached, Ella walked over to take her food out of the microwave. She noticed Zach was staring at her very intently, but she didn't say anything. By this time, Zach had been part of the team for several months and had begun to realize that he wanted to learn more about the culture of his coworkers. Unfortunately, he chose Ella to be his cultural adviser, and she wasn't interested in anything except making him look foolish every chance she got.

Pretending not to notice Zach, Ella took her food out of the microwave, sat at her desk, and closed her eyes as she quietly said grace before eating. She opened her eyes to find Zach sitting across from her. *This white boy is about to ask me something stupid,* she thought.

"Hey, Ella, can I ask you a question? What do you say when you bless your food?"

Annoyed that her thoughts were correct, Ella replied, "I just ask God to bless the food."

Zach slid his chair closer. "Yeah, but what do you actually say?"

Devin overheard the conversation and paused what he was doing to listen to Ella's response, knowing she wouldn't pass up the opportunity to lead Zach down a rabbit hole.

Ella smiled. "You know what? I'm glad you asked. I normally say the alphabet."

"The alphabet? What do you mean?" Zach asked.

"Yeah, I try to say a prayer that starts with every letter of the alphabet. Something like 'All Blessings Come Down Eternally, and … Forever Good' A, B, C, D, E, F, G. And so forth until I get to Z."

"Whoa, that's serious. I had no idea you were so spiritual," Zach said as he slowly sat back in his chair.

Devin shook his head in disbelief as he pretended to use the copy machine.

As Devin struggled to hold back his laughter, the office door opened, and Agent Sparks walked into the detachment, fresh from his TDY to Busan. As usual, the room lit up when Sparks walked in and greeted everyone, but he was caught off guard by Ella's remarks.

"What's up, Al? You look like you've been up to some shenanigans."

No one would have paid any attention to Ella, but Sparks seemed paralyzed by her statement, and for some reason unknown to Devin and Zach, Sparks had a very guilty look on his face. Zach took interest in Sparks's reaction and peeked over at Devin to see if he noticed the same. Ella continued to stare at Sparks, waiting several seconds for a reaction, but none came. He just stood there as if she caught him eating her dessert she had stashed in the refrigerator.

Finally, Sparks was saved from embarrassment when the office phone began to ring. Zach answered the phone and looked shocked by what he was told. He checked the time on his watch and hung up the call.

"Hey, that was Detective Kim. Apparently, the girl we met last night walked up to TSGT Cochran from Town Patrol and handed him my card. I need to go check this out. Anybody wanna roll?"

Devin quickly agreed to go with Zach, but Sparks declined. "Nah, fellas, sorry, I already made plans for lunch. Hey, DJ, did anything develop from our visit to the pharmacy?"

Devin and Zach began to laugh as they walked out the door. "Nah, nothing much, only an attempted murder case. I'll tell you about it later, bruh," Devin responded.

Devin and Zachary drove up to the main gate, parked their vehicle inside the base, and walked out of the pedestrian exit. They immediately saw Detective Kim, Samantha, and TSGT Cochran waiting for them. Cochran explained that Samantha had approached him with Agent Zachary's business card and said she needed to speak with him. The agents thanked Cochran for calling them, and he walked away to resume his duties at the gate.

"Samantha, what's going on? Are you okay?" Zach asked.

Samantha looked fine, but her behavior suggested that she was very anxious about something. "Yes, I'm fine. You helped me last night, so I wanted to show you something. Come with me; we must go quickly."

The agents and Detective Kim followed Samantha down the main thoroughfare of the entertainment district, then along side streets until they found themselves standing in an alleyway behind an old warehouse, roughly fifteen minutes from the main gate to Osan.

When they arrived at the location, Samantha pulled a paper bag out of a half-full trash can. She stuck her hand inside the bag and held out the contents to Zach. "Here. This is what they give us."

Zach looked down and saw Samantha handing him a syringe half-filled with a clear liquid. "What is that?"

Samantha shook her head. "I don't know exactly what's in the syringe, but whatever it is, it always makes the girls extremely drowsy." She explained that the bar owners usually gave it to the new girls because they would have a hard time understanding that they were not brought to Korea to become singers but to sell their bodies.

Zach shook his head in disbelief. "So they're drugging you to keep you from running away."

Samantha's eyes began to fill with tears. "That's not all," she said. "After they stick you with the needle, they do things to you. The old men—they come and do things to the girls while they are sleeping."

While Zach was speaking to Samantha, Devin heard noises coming from the second floor of the old warehouse. He noticed the rusty fire escape attached to the building and decided to see if he could figure out the source of the noises. He climbed the fire escape and found an old door that was cracked open. Devin knew he shouldn't enter the building, but he couldn't understand why those sounds would be coming from inside an abandoned warehouse. Against his better judgment, he gently pulled the door open and stepped into the near-complete darkness. Instantly, he was met with a rotting smell. The sound of water dripping down from the ceiling onto the concrete floor broke the silence between the moans. A few feet in, Devin paused and debated whether to keep going. He heard more moans and decided to push forward.

As he drew closer to the noise, Devin pulled his pistol from its holster. With his free hand, he took out a tactical flashlight and aimed it toward the source of the clanging noise. Back on the street, Agent Zachary was not happy that Devin entered the building alone and nodded to Detective Kim to go in after him.

As Agent Jackson walked further into the darkness, he could hardly believe what he saw. The beam from his flashlight illuminated several large steel cages. As he got closer, he noticed women sleeping inside each one, lying on small blow-up mattresses on the floor. Some were still dressed in the clothes they had on when they arrived in Korea. As he guided the light through the warehouse, he saw empty syringes scattered across the cage floors. A water hose snaked its way from the wall, which the girls used to pass around for water. Inside each cage was a bucket for the women to relieve themselves. Devin stood almost paralyzed by what he was seeing, but his attention was abruptly diverted when he heard a cracking sound, as if someone had stepped on a piece of glass. He found himself holding his breath, listening more intently and to ensure he wasn't imagining things. But then he heard footsteps.

Devin instantly recognized the noise as someone walking in his direction. He quickly turned off his flashlight, but in the darkness, he couldn't find a good hiding place. Stumbling over items on the floor, he took cover beside what he thought was a wall locker. The footsteps grew closer. The unknown person turned on a flashlight and seemed to be looking for someone.

Unbeknownst to Devin, Detective Kim had entered the building and was slowly making her way toward his position. Devin, believing the kidnappers had returned and found him snooping around, had only a moment to decide what to do.

He chose to act. He couldn't bear the thought of waiting to be shot, so he raised his pistol and tried to take aim at the unknown figure. Devin slid his finger onto the trigger of his weapon and began to control his breathing. He stared intently at the glowing front sight of his Sig Sauer pistol and began to slowly squeeze the trigger, reducing the slack, while aiming at the faint light approaching him.

Suddenly, the unknown person walked through a sliver of sunlight filtering through a covered window, revealing that it was Detective Kim. She froze at once, realizing that the muzzle of a gun was just two feet from her face. Kim wasn't immediately sure it was Devin holding the weapon. She braced herself, waiting for the flash, but, thankfully, it never came.

Devin slowly lowered his weapon and stepped into the beam of light to reveal himself to Detective Kim. Relieved, she grabbed his shoulder with her right hand and leaned against the wall.

Before Devin could say anything, he was cut off by the sound of a door opening at the other end of the floor. Devin quickly pulled Kim into the shadows with him. The two heard footsteps and what sounded like two men speaking. The bar owner had returned to check on the girls and was giving a tour of the facility to Mr. Kovalenko.

"So, as you can see, we have tightened our security on the girls. You don't have to worry about another one getting out of her ... accommodations," the owner said.

Kovalenko, though displeased to be in the warehouse, knew he had to keep the Koreans on their toes to ensure the operation continued smoothly. He shone a flashlight around the floor and, for the first time, saw the horrid conditions in which the girls were kept.

"Good God, what is going on in here? What is that smell? Don't tell me that's coming from the bathroom," he said.

The Korean bar owner laughed. "Bathroom? No, there is no bathroom. We give them all buckets, and they can dump them every night on their way to work."

Kovalenko walked up to one of the cages and shone his light on a girl who had passed out from being drugged. Oblivious to how the girls were treated, he inquired about their health. "What's wrong with this one?" Kovalenko asked.

The bar owner explained that there was nothing wrong with the girl, but that she had passed out from the injection he gave her to calm her nerves after she first arrived. Kovalenko was shocked by the Korean's response and directed him to unlock the girl's cage.

Kovalenko walked into the cage, kneeled beside her, and grabbed her hand. While the girl was still sleeping, Kovalenko dipped his handkerchief into the water and wiped the sweat from her face. "I know you've been doing this for a long time, but this is barbaric. It's sad to see what humans will do to one another. Her own people sold her here. Now I facilitate it to protect my people. There is nothing inside of me that says this is okay, but if I don't do it, then it will be my people locked up in cages."

Kovalenko laid the girl's head back down on her mattress and left the building with the bar owner. Devin and Kim listened to their footsteps and the door closing behind them. Devin quickly pulled out his cell phone and took pictures of the girls in their cages. Detective Kim, furious as Devin was taking pictures instead of helping her break the locks on the cages, demanded, "What are you doing? Help me get them out of here!"

Devin slowly looked away and shook his head. "I can't," he said. "This is clearly an issue for the Korean police, and my country ass ain't supposed to be in here."

Detective Kim was not happy with his response.

"Look, Kim, if we don't do this the right way, we'll only make the problem worse. Yeah, we might be able to help these few girls, but we won't affect the system that's doing this. We've got to get the right people involved."

Furious with Devin's logic, Detective Kim quickly turned and walked back toward the exit. As they climbed down the fire escape, they saw that Zach and Samantha had finished their conversation and that Samantha was heading away on her own.

"What's up? Find anything good?" Zach asked.

Devin stood emotionless and turned to Detective Kim, who seemed to be wiping a tear from her cheek. She pushed past Zach, walked out of the alley, and disappeared into the crowd in the entertainment district. Zach, confused by Detective Kim's attitude, asked Devin, "What happened inside the building?"

"We need to get back and brief the boss immediately," Devin responded, still trying to come to grips with what he had just witnessed.

Devin and Zachary returned to the detachment, called all the agents into the conference room, and showed them the pictures of the caged girls. Just then, Detective Kim walked in, still furious with Devin. She looked over and saw the photos on the table and calmed down, realizing the agents were going to move swiftly to help the girls.

Agent Zachary explained to Agent Chang how the girls were recruited, held against their will, and forced into prostitution as their only means of leaving Korea and returning to the Philippines. Agent Chang, who was somewhat risk-averse, didn't like the idea of briefing the Wing Commander that his airmen were aiding and abetting human trafficking. He turned to Detective Kim for advice. "What does the KNP know about this?"

Kim responded, "To be honest, we've known about it for a while but were unable to stop it. The province has a business agreement with the airbase. As long as airmen are visiting the local businesses, the business owners agree not to protest the base. When we tried to investigate the issue, the businesses threatened massive protests, which would have caused the base to shut down the gates, and the legit business owners would go out of business."

Agent Chang began to quickly talk himself into making the right decision. "We've got to do something! The Wing Commander will be hesitant to risk a riot based on these photos, but I think we should push this up to JAG at USFK. We're gonna need more photos and a clear picture of who's involved."

Agent Mullins chimed in, saying the team needed to get the KNP involved at once. Detective Kim agreed to brief her province commander and contact the local magistrate to begin working on the search warrants immediately.

As the plan began to unfold, Agent Chang handed out assignments: "Zach, get on the phone with Yokota and tell the tech guys we need an assist. Sparks, you and Devin go brief the Wing Jag; let them know this has to be a priority for the commander, and we need it pushed to USFK immediately."

The team agreed and hurriedly exited to carry out their assignments.

As the agents disbursed, Agent Mullins pulled Zach aside. "Hey, excellent work out there. Where was Sparks?"

"I don't know. He said he had lunch plans."

Agent Mullins looked a bit confused as to why Sparks didn't join his team on the source meet. She thanked Agent Zachary and walked back into her office.

Two days later, the tech agents from Yokota Airbase in Japan arrived at Osan. After unloading their gear, the team assembled in the detachment conference room for a mission brief from Agent Chang.

"Gentlemen, thanks for flying out. We need immediate assistance from your expertise. We've come to learn that many of the establishments frequented by our airmen are engaging in human trafficking. From a foreign military standpoint, all we can do is place those establishments off-limits to GIs and hope they go out of business. But, with the help of the Korean National Police, we can conduct joint operations to rescue those women. Agent Zachary will get you up to speed, and the sooner we can get those cameras in place, the sooner we can get those girls home."

The tech agents were eager to help with the operation. They were even more excited to see their training finally pay off on a mission that would save lives instead of just capturing images of dependents stealing equipment from the base gym.

After the meeting, the agents decided to treat the Yokota crew to a Korean dinner in Songtan. It had been snowing for the past two days, so they grabbed their jackets and headed for the door. On the way out, Devin noticed Ella Mae still working at her desk. "Hey, Ella, you riding with us or what?" he asked.

"Nah, not this time, DJ. I've got to get this evidence inventory done by tomorrow. If I finish up in time, I might try to meet you guys a little later," Ella responded.

Devin paused as he realized that Ella had been asked to take on the evidence program to alleviate some of the workload from the agents, and now they were going out to have a good time while she was being left behind in the detachment. Devin took off his jacket and sat down on the corner of Ella's desk. "No worries. I'll stay and help you out, especially since a lot of that stuff came from my black-market case."

Surprised by the gesture, Ella saw this as an opportunity to get Devin's attention. She thanked him for staying and reached out to touch his hand. Just as she did, Agent Mullins poked her head around the corner. "Jackson! Let's go," she yelled, aggressively motioning for him to leave the office with her.

"I was going to stay behind and help out with the evidence inventory," he said.

"No, I need you with us. Ella's a big girl; she can manage it by herself. Come on, we're leaving now!"

Devin turned to Ella to apologize, but before he could say anything, Ella grabbed his hand. "It's okay, DJ. I appreciate the offer anyway. I'll see you tomorrow. Have a good night."

Devin nodded and quickly left the building, leaving his jacket hanging on the back of his chair.

After about two hours of reviewing evidence and matching log numbers to the inventory sheet, Ella felt the need to stretch her legs. It was clear to her that no one was coming back that night to help her, so she decided to do a little snooping around on the agent's desks—and inside the drawers. She walked back to the bullpen, always intimidated by the stacks of papers and random notes scribbled on yellow sticky pads stuck to the dividing walls of their cubicles. She walked to the rear of the room and began to hover over Detective Kim's desk. Most of the documents were written in Korean, but she became fixated on a pair of sunglasses with lightly brown-tinted lenses. She slid the glasses on her face and walked over to the mirror to see if the eyewear made her look like a cop. Ella liked the fresh look, but she wasn't satisfied.

Next, she went over to Agent Sparks's desk and removed his shoulder holster from the back of his chair. She took it over to the mirror but had no idea how to put it on. Once she figured out which loops to put her arms through, she still thought it was on incorrectly because it looked so big on her petite torso. Still not done, Ella made her way over to Agent Zachary's desk. She was looking for something specific but didn't immediately see it. She hesitated for a moment, looked around the room out of guilt, and then opened his top drawer. Knowing that Zach was a Krav Maga instructor, she had seen one of his dummy weapons before in the office. She reached into the drawer and pulled out a blue plastic gun that she held onto as though it were a live weapon. Ella carefully walked back over to the mirror with the gun in her hand and was shocked to see that the plastic gun fit into Sparks's shoulder rig. She practiced drawing her weapon in the mirror, dropping the gun on the floor multiple times because her hands were too small to hold it while removing it from the holster.

While staring at her reflection, she saw Devin's leather jacket across the room. Again, she looked around the room before putting it on. As soon as she pulled it up over the shoulder rig, she got an instant whiff of Devin's cologne. Now she felt complete, as in her eyes, she had captured the essence of each of the agents: Detective Kim's focus, the blue gun representing Zach's tactical skills, the physical strength from Sparks's shoulder holster, and Devin's coolness. She grabbed her cell phone and began taking selfies in the mirror. As she was posing and imitating 1970s female crime fighters, she noticed Agent Mullins staring at her in the mirror. She turned around and quickly took off the sunglasses. Ella was so embarrassed she couldn't speak. Agent Mullins slowly walked up to her with a disgusted look on her face.

"If you really want to know what it's like, put in an application and find out."

Ella began to take off the borrowed items as Mullins turned to walk to her office, laughing.

"If you join, you're gonna need a much smaller shoulder rig." Mullins closed her office door behind her.

Ella removed the last of her borrowed "agent attire" and sat back down at her desk, too ashamed to look toward Mullins office. Although she dreaded the forthcoming laughter from the agents once they heard about her office shenanigans, she couldn't help but smile to herself, thinking about what her future might look like if she became an agent.

That weekend was mostly uneventful for the agents, as the tech guys from Yokota were collaborating with their Korean counterparts to install cameras in the suspected hotspots off-base. The following morning, Devin invited the team out for lunch. Zach and Ella agreed to join, but Sparks declined the invitation. As soon as he did, Zach gave Devin a worried glance. Devin had no idea what was bothering Zach. Just then, Sparks's cell phone began to ring; he looked down to identify the caller but didn't answer. Once again, Zach gave a quick glance at Devin. Ella noticed the glances and turned to Devin to figure out what the problem was. Devin, still oblivious to Zach's concerns, shrugged and turned back around to his computer.

About a minute later, Sparks's cell phone rang again. "Alex, you gonna get that?" Zach asked. Sparks looked over at Zach, then picked up his phone and walked out of the building.

By this point in the tour, Zach had grown close to Sparks, enough to know when something odd was happening. He walked over to Devin's cubicle and poked his head over the divider. "DJ, man, you got a sec? I think we have a problem."

Without looking away from his computer screen, Devin replied, "Problem? What do you mean?"

Zach looked down the hallway to ensure Agent Mullins wasn't within earshot of the conversation. "I think there's something going on with Alex."

Devin slowly turned to Zach, raising an eyebrow. Zach continued. "For the past few weeks, he's been acting really strange. Like just now, he wouldn't answer the phone. Someone has been calling him since before his trip to Busan, and whenever I've been around, he won't answer the call."

Devin laughed. "Come on, man. Maybe it's just some chick he's messing with."

Zach nodded and leaned in closer. "Nah, I wish it was. Yesterday, Agent Yang called from the Busan detachment. I asked him how he liked working with Al, and he said he hasn't seen Al!"

"What? He said he went down there for work."

Zachary backed away and begin to move toward his desk. "Exactly."

CHAPTER 6
TARGET FILE

After catching up with their paperwork, Devin and Sparks headed to the JAG office to meet with Capt. Murphy. As they rounded the corner, she greeted them with a huge smile. "Hey, it's my favorite Bad Boys!" Captain Murphy laughed at her own joke while the two agents looked at each other and shook their heads—obviously this wasn't the first time they had heard the comparison.

"What's good, Cap?" Sparks asked as he took a seat in front of her desk. "We just wanna get you caught up with what's happening."

Capt. Murphy sat back in her chair and prepared to listen intently.

Devin leaned back against the wall with his hands in his pockets. "We're about to kick off an operation targeting human trafficking right outside the base. We're gonna need your assistance to get the Wing Commander's attention and get USFK on board."

Capt. Murphy looked a bit confused. "Human trafficking? Yeah, absolutely. I thought you guys were here to talk about oxycodone."

Sparks returned the confused look. "What oxycodone?"

"The oxy that's missing from the base pharmacy," she replied. Capt. Murphy laughed as she realized that she had attained significant criminal information before OSI was aware of it.

As the two agents walked back to the vehicle, they both seemed a bit embarrassed that Capt. Murphy seemed to have a leg up on them regarding the missing oxy. Sparks sat in the driver's seat and paused before starting the car. "Didn't we just visit the pharmacy not too long ago?"

Devin, looking straight ahead, nodded. "Yep, and that goofy ass Tech Sergeant didn't say shit about missing oxy. Bruh, I knew something was off the whole time we were in that office. We gotta find a way to catch up!" Devin turned his head to stare out of the passenger side window, contemplating their next steps. "I think I have a plan," he said as Sparks reversed the car out of the parking lot.

Later that night, around 8:30 p.m., Isabella, the Staff Sergeant from the base pharmacy who had become the target of Ramirez's continued sexual harassment, exited her dormitory and walked to the covered bus stop at the edge of the parking lot. As she walked from the building, she turned heads, dressed in an extremely low-cut blouse that was missing the two top buttons. Her short skirt was so tight that she had a hard time walking. Even though there was about two feet of snow on the ground, she chose not to wear a coat because she wasn't going to pass up what she believed was an opportunity to get what—and who—she wanted.

Isabella waited nervously and kept checking her watch. The base community bus pulled into the parking lot and stopped about three feet away from the covered bus stop. When the vehicle stopped, the driver opened the door and saw Isabella standing there, dressed as though she were heading out for a night in Las Vegas. Before he could gather his thoughts, Isabella waved him off to signal that she was waiting for someone else. Disappointed, the bus driver closed the door and eased the bus back onto the road. As the bus exited the parking lot, Isabella spotted a car pulling up with dark-tinted windows. The mysterious car pulled to the side of the road across from the bus stop, and suddenly the driver's window began to lower. Isabella, staring intently at the vehicle, recognized Devin as the driver. The two locked eyes, and Devin motioned for Isabella to join him inside the vehicle. Isabella turned around to pick up her purse from the bench, adjusting her top to show even more cleavage, then turned and seductively walked around the rear of Devin's car. She opened the front passenger door to find Sparks sitting there with an extremely agitated look on his face.

"If you don't get your ass in the back seat!" Sparks shouted.

Isabella was not thrilled that Sparks had joined their meeting—and even less pleased that he was not impressed with her choice of outfit for the night. She rolled her eyes, slammed his door shut, and sat in the back seat of the vehicle. Devin pulled the car back onto the road, and the three headed to a desolate area in the rear of the airbase, behind the runways. Because there wasn't much traffic in this part of the base, roughly three feet of snow had built up alongside the road. In the agents' minds, this was a suitable place to meet with an informant as there were no lights and no reason for anyone to be there. The vehicle stopped, and the three exited, standing in the middle of the road, which had about two inches of snow after the snowplows had been through. Isabella reached into her purse, pulled out several pages of documents, and handed them to Devin. Using the light from his cell phone, he reviewed the documents but wasn't sure what he was looking at.

"What's this telling me?" Devin asked Isabella as he handed the papers back to her. She grabbed the light from Devin's hands and began to explain the data.

"That's the pharmacy inventory list for the past three months. If you look at the highlighted area, you'll see that every other week the hillbilly heroin is coming up short."

Sparks tilted his head, trying to decipher what Isabella was referring to. "Hillbilly heroin? What the hell is that?"

"Oxycodone" Devin replied.

"Bingo, you win first prize!" Isabella joked as she handed the paperwork to Sparks, who began to review the data and asked who was responsible for conducting the inventory. Isabella thought for a second, then responded, "Well, Tech Sergeant Wilson is responsible for reporting the numbers, but he has Staff Sergeant Ramirez actually conduct the audit."

Sparks immediately responded, "Ramirez? Isn't he the guy that…"

"Bingo! Devin interrupted.

Sparks and Devin stared at each other, both nodding as they silently acknowledged their next steps without saying too much in front of Isabella. "Alright, I guess we're done. Let's go," Devin said.

As the three walked back toward the vehicle, Sparks took one last jab at Osan's beauty queen. "Hey, Isabella, you did a good job. You wanna sit in the front seat?"

Not amused by Sparks's sarcasm and upset that she didn't get what she wanted from Devin, she flipped Sparks off and continued walking back to the car. Sparks laughed. "What? I was trying to be nice to your thirsty ass!"

After the meeting, Devin dropped Sparks off at the apartment building and visited a bar alone to blow off some steam. He was having a tough time dealing with the images of the girls locked in their cages and couldn't help but think he should have done more at the moment to help them. Although he knew he made the right decision because of jurisdiction, he feared that the Air Force would shy away from the problem and label it as a "Korean issue."

Ella and her girlfriends got together that night to celebrate one of their birthdays by going out to a jazz bar. Upon entering the establishment, Ella noticed Devin sitting alone in the corner. She didn't want to bother him in case he was expecting company, but she could tell something was off with his demeanor. She walked over and tried to gauge his mood without making the situation worse.

"What's up, stranger? Whatcha doing here by yourself? You waiting for someone?" she asked.

"Nah, it's just me tonight. I'm just chillin'," he replied.

"Oh, okay. Well, I'll let you go. See you at work tomorrow." Ella began to walk away and headed toward her friends' table. She turned around again and realized she didn't like the feeling she got from Devin, so she returned to his table.

"Hey, let me buy you a drink. You look like you need one."

"Thanks, El."

Ella signaled for the waitress to bring two beers, then sat down at his table. When she did, Devin couldn't help but notice how beautiful she looked that night. He had obviously seen her out of uniform many times before, but there was something different about her that night. Ella wore a fluffy white sweater that was cut right above her belly button. Her tight skirt seemed to perfectly accentuate her thin hips, and her thin gold ankle bracelet matched her necklace, which had a diamond pendant with her initial "E." She didn't believe in wearing a lot of makeup, nor did she need to, but that night she could have given Queen Nefertiti a run for her money. She had tried several times before to get Devin to notice her, but on this night, she succeeded.

"So, you wanna tell me what's got you in this funk?" she asked.

Devin shook his head. "Nothing specific. Just the job wearing on me a bit."

Ella smirked and lightly punched Devin's shoulder. "What are you talking about? You guys are killing it! All three of you."

Devin paused for a second, then looked Ella in the eyes, "Yeah, it's just … some of this stuff can be heavy. Every day we deal with someone having the worst day of their life. Either they got raped, robbed, assaulted, or somebody tried to kill them. Then they come to us, and we have to make them relive the event all over again, every single detail. Don't get me wrong, sometimes when I finish those interviews, my next thought is about food, or I'm laughing at one of your jokes, but sometimes the darkness that's on some of those people gets transferred to us. And they expect us to be Superman every day and not let it bother us. I mean, I get it, but sometimes it can be a little too much."

Slow jazz played softly in the dimly lit bar. Ella wanted to be sympathetic to what Devin was explaining to her, but she couldn't help but smile as he began to open up to her. "Well, you know you can rely on your team. Those guys have your back, DJ."

"Yeah, I know. I'm lucky to be able to learn from them."

Ella put her hand on top of his and smiled. "I'm lucky just to be around you guys. All three of you … especially you."

Devin was caught off guard and turned toward Ella. "El, what are you saying?"

She shook her head in disappointment. "Dang, for a federal agent, it sure takes you a long time to figure out who's got a crush on you."

Normally, Ella would have let out a huge laugh after that type of statement, but her heart was beating so fast she could barely breathe. This time, she just stared at Devin in silence.

"El ... see, I don't know when you're joking or not," Devin said as he tried to fully comprehend the moment. He wanted it to be real, but he understood that Ella could break out in laughter at any moment. To show that she was expressing her true feelings, she slowly leaned over to Devin and gently kissed him on his lips. As she pulled away, Devin's eyes were locked on hers.

"Did that seem like a joke to you?" she asked nervously, breaking eye contact.

Devin moved in closer to Ella and whispered in her ear, "Are you sure this is what you want?"

"Yes."

Devin and Ella left the bar together and found themselves on the rooftop of the jazz bar. They were always relaxed around each other, and now that they'd made their feelings known, they seemed even closer. Devin appeared to be in a much better place mentally as he leaned against the railing and looked over the edge. He stared into the night sky as Ella slid close behind him and worked her hands under his jacket to give him a big embrace. She was met with a huge surprise as she mistakenly grabbed his gun resting in his shoulder holster.

"Devin! When I decided to give you a hug, I didn't think I'd end up with a handful of pistol. Ha!!"

Devin laughed as he looked over his shoulder at Ella, whose eyes appeared to be glowing in the moonlight. "Well, maybe you should go a little lower."

Intrigued by the proposition, Ella released the gun and worked her hands down Devin's torso. "What the hell!" Ella immediately pulled her hands away. "Handcuffs, DJ?"

"Hey, be careful with those."

Ella looked back at Devin with a playful side eye. "Really? Now why would I want your handcuffs … wait, what am I saying?" The two continued to laugh together and decided to continue their night at Ella's apartment.

Inside Ella's place, they sat on the couch to watch a movie, but it didn't take long before their lips were touching. As Ella pushed Devin backward onto the couch, she got nervous and excused herself to use the restroom. Devin could sense Ella's hesitation. She closed the bathroom door behind her, removed her earrings, and tried to convince herself that this moment was real. She nervously knocked one of the earrings onto the rug and tried to bend over to pick it up, but her skirt was so tight that she couldn't make it down to the floor on the first try. She rocked back and forth a few times until she finally reached the earring.

Unbeknownst to Ella, the bathroom door had crept open, catching Devin's attention. He focused on her just as she was shimmying back and forth and assumed that she was in the bathroom twerking. Devin jumped up from the couch and tried to process what he had just witnessed. *She's in there twerking? Dang, she 'bout to put that thang on me!* The last thing he wanted to do was not live up to the moment, so he quickly hit the floor to knock out a quick set of push-ups to get his blood flowing. … eight

... nine ... ten. When he rose to his feet, he felt a sharp pinch in his lower back.

No, no, no, no, no ... not now! Not tonight, don't do this! He thought if he stretched his back, he might prevent it from getting any worse. He placed his right hand on his hip, lunged forward with his left leg, and grabbed the couch with his other hand in an attempt to stretch out the muscles in his lower back.

Just then, Ella opened the bathroom door and caught an obstructed view of what appeared to be Devin doing pelvic thrusts against the couch. She immediately closed the door and walked back to the mirror.

Oh no! He's about to tear my ass up! Why was he thrusting so hard? I don't know ... I don't think I'm ready for all this. After a few moments of staring at her reflection and accepting how beautiful she looked that night, she undid a couple of buttons on her blouse and winked at herself in the mirror before exiting the bathroom and returning to the living room. When she returned, she found Devin sitting on the edge of the couch. She plopped down on the cushion beside him, and the two sat in awkward silence. Devin looked around the room for something to talk about, but all he could think about was Ella's hips gyrating in a way that he never would have imagined. Ella, eager to restart the conversation, said the first thing that came to mind.

"So, you like humping couches ... yeah, that's cool."

"What?" Before Devin could fully respond, he realized what she must have seen from the bathroom and began laughing with her. He grabbed the throw pillow and playfully hit her in the face. Instead of being upset, Ella felt a sense of relief. Although she had thought about this moment for quite some time, she felt the night had begun to move a little too quickly for her. However, she was willing to follow through if it was what Devin wanted. Feeling relaxed, she grabbed a blanket and curled up next to him on the couch. After realizing that they both were a bit nervous, they ended up watching movies until they fell asleep on the couch together.

Later in the week, the Osan JAG office finally had an opportunity to brief the airbase commander, Brigadier General Lane, a decorated F-16 fighter pilot, about the proposed operation from the OSI Office. General Lane was not eager to have Air Force agents so involved in off-base operations in Korea, but the thought that his airmen may have unknowingly contributed to a human trafficking network was too much for him to swallow—especially if the media found out that he knew about it and did nothing to rescue the victims. Eager to pass the problem on to United States Forces Korea Headquarters, he picked up the phone and called the Diplomatic Relations office at USFK headquarters. This office was occupied by US Embassy personnel who would collaborate directly with military leaders and push for non-military solutions on the peninsula. Whenever military officers needed to find a way around a potential civic disaster, they would happily call the Diplomatic Relations office to dump the responsibility off on the State Department.

The phone rang twice in the office and was picked up by the director. "Diplomatic Relations Office, Viktor Kovalenko speaking. How may I help you?"

General Lane introduced himself to Kovalenko and began to explain the reason for his call. "I've got a situation that has developed outside of our airbase. Some of our OSI agents have uncovered what they believe is a large human trafficking network. That's bad enough, but it's worse when our airmen are the ones frequenting these locations and basically are the reason the girls are brought here. So, what do you guys suggest we do about it? OSI wants to go in and shut it down, but this ain't America—we can't just do what we want. So, what does the State Department recommend?"

While General Lane was speaking, Kovalenko began to sweat profusely. He wasn't sure if this was actually a call for help or if OSI already had knowledge of his involvement and was working to trap him into making a statement. Either way, he figured he would be best served by trying to downplay the situation. "General, first, thanks for calling me, and yes, I am aware of this issue. I can assure you that we are working to solve it through diplomatic channels with the South Korean government. So, there's no need for the agents to get involved in this one. We need to tread carefully on this issue. But you have my word. It will be taken care of."

General Lane welcomed Kovalenko's answer and saw an opening to completely wash his hands of the situation. "That's what I needed to hear. Do you want me to send up the evidence that OSI collected?"

"Evidence? What evidence?" Kovalenko asked.

"They've got video of these poor girls locked in cages and the drugs they used to sedate them."

Kovalenko wondered if any of the evidence could have pointed toward him. "OSI has that? Ah, no, no need to send it to me. We will get it taken care of. Thank you, General."

Kovalenko slowly hung up the phone and sat in silence for the next few minutes. After devising his next step, he barked orders at his secretary. "Sheryll, have them pull my car around. I need to make a trip down to Songtan."

At around 1900 hours, several of the bar owners were meeting in one of the nightclubs before the establishments opened for the evening. They were discussing the delay in oxycodone and when they could expect the next round of girls to arrive from the Philippines. One of the bar owners, Mr. Suh, who owned the nightclub "The Rebound," said that he had received a call earlier that morning from Manila and that fifteen new girls had signed contracts so far that month. The girls were expected to be in Korea within the next two weeks. Another owner, Mr. Cho, was not satisfied with only fifteen new girls and questioned Mr. Suh about the lack of oxycodone. "When will we get more? I'm losing money."

Suddenly, Staff Sgt. Ramirez stepped out of the shadows from behind the bar. "Don't worry. Everything is under control.

Those who wish to stop us have other things they need to worry about right now."

As soon as Ramirez seemed to gain the trust of the Korean bar owners, the front door flung open, and Viktor Kovalenko walked in. He was still wearing his suit from his job at the USFK. In fact, he left in such a hurry that his security badge was still clipped to his jacket lapel. "What is this shit I hear about OSI taking video of the girls? And that they recovered the drugs ... Somebody better start talking!" screamed Kovalenko.

Mr. Cho stood up. "Viktor, I don't know what you're talking about. Who has video? I've not seen any video."

Kovalenko began to slowly encircle the table where the owners were sitting. "I got a call today from the Wing Commander asking what to do about the trafficking problem. I managed to calm him down for now, but it's only a matter of time before they'll want to push the issue again. So, from now on, you bitches better run a tight ship, or I'll sink it myself!" Kovalenko clapped his hands twice and the bar was flooded from both entrances with hitmen from the Ukrainian mafia. "Do I make myself clear?"

"Yes, Viktor," Mr. Cho responded.

Kovalenko turned and noticed Staff Sgt. Ramirez standing in the corner. "What's your punk ass doing here? Shouldn't you be getting me more product?"

Ramirez, who had been quiet until this moment, stepped forward and responded, "Yeah, I'm on top of that. But I think I have a solution to our problem."

Kovalenko looked very unsatisfied and rolled his eyes. "You better not be talking about another rat."

Ramirez laughed. "No sir, no rats. This time it's rat poison."

Several blocks away from where the bar owners were meeting, Devin and Ella were having dinner together at a local Italian restaurant. The restaurant was located on the second floor of the building, and their table was directly against the balcony overlooking the main entrance to the entertainment district. As the two were finishing their meal, Ella started to feel a bit antsy. She was thrilled that she and Devin had been spending so much time together, but she couldn't help but wonder about the other woman, Tori. Was she a threat? Could she become the other woman? Or was Ella herself the other woman? She began to get lost in her thoughts so much that Devin noticed she had become quiet and stopped eating her food.

"Ella, seems like something is bothering you. What's going on?" he asked.

At first, Ella nodded and turned her head away from him, but seeing that Devin didn't seem too fazed by her attitude, she decided to press him on the situation. "So, you gonna tell me who she is?"

"Who, who is?" Devin responded.

Ella didn't seem amused that Devin wasn't reading her mind. "That girl that spoke to you at the club."

Finally sensing the tension, Devin sat back in his chair. "Yeah, that's Tori. We used to be tight a few years ago."

Ella tried to hide her concern and looked down at her phone before responding, "What do you mean by that?"

"She and I dated for about a year and a half before I joined OSI."

"So, what happened to you guys?" Ella asked.

"She decided she didn't want to have a long-distance relationship. Especially with a Fed," Devin said.

Ella rolled her eyes and took another bite from her plate. "Oh, I see, so you chose your job over your girlfriend?"

Devin really didn't want to break down the failures of his previous romance to Ella, especially early in their relationship. But he knew that if she was asking, then she must have been thinking about it for some time. "Nah, that's not exactly how it happened."

Ella nodded for him to continue.

"Look, Tori and I had started getting serious right before I got accepted into OSI. Although I still enjoyed working on the jets, I didn't think it was something I wanted to do for the rest of my life. I saw OSI as a chance to reset and do something that could lead to another career, you know, after the Air Force. So, to be honest, one reason I joined was to be as cool as the dudes in the movies—yeah, I know, don't laugh—and the other reason was to try and make a better future for me and Tori. Unfortunately, she didn't stay around long enough for me to tell her that."

Ella didn't bat an eye and was eager to continue to press Devin for information. "Oh, but she's back now?"

"Nah, I didn't even know she was here until that night. Why? Are you trying to size up the competition?"

Ella laughed nervously. "Ha! Please, there is no competition. Ha!"

As they were laughing, Ella spotted Sparks walking alone through the district. He was dressed conservatively and wore a hat pulled down over his eyes. "DJ, check it out—your boy's up to something," Ella said.

Devin looked out the window and spotted his partner acting very suspiciously. "Come on now, El. I still think he's probably just sneaking around with some chick. Probably somebody we both know, and he's trying to keep it from us, like the lady at the ADAPT office that he thinks I don't know about."

Recalling the feeling she had a few nights ago while posing in the mirror, Ella challenged Devin to dig deeper. "Well, there's only one way to know." She slowly stood and picked up her purse, signaling for Devin to join her.

They quickly paid for their meals and left the restaurant to follow Sparks. They trailed from a distance as Devin recognized that Sparks was using counter-surveillance techniques as he traversed the district.

Sparks walked into a long alley. Once he got halfway down, he turned back in the direction he came from, seemingly checking to see if he was being followed. Devin and Ella were almost caught as they were at the entrance to the alley when Sparks began to backtrack. The two quickly ducked into a store to hide until Sparks had cleared the area. To Ella, this was just a fun adventure, but Devin began to wonder why Sparks was so eager to cover his tracks.

Sparks ventured further into the entertainment district, eventually walking into the outdoor seafood market, which was crowded with customers. At that point, Devin and Ella lost sight of him. They decided to split up to find Sparks. Devin walked around the north end of the market while Ella headed in the opposite direction. After five minutes, there was still no sign of him. Suddenly, Sparks was standing face-to-face with Ella.

"Ella, what are you doing way out here by yourself?" Sparks asked, looking around to see if she was actually alone.

Before she could answer, Devin appeared from a crowd of customers only a few feet away from Sparks, who stood there looking rather perplexed. "DJ? Wait … y'all out here together?"

"Ahh, yeah," Ella responded. "We were trying to find that new seafood restaurant—you know, the one with the giant eel or something. You said you didn't wanna go … so …."

Sparks looked around, eager to find an excuse to end the conversation. "Yeah, nah, that's cool. Well, alright, I'll let y'all get to it."

Sparks gave Devin a pound and began to walk away. "Alright, cool, man. Catch you later."

Devin and Ella walked off, letting Sparks continue through the market. After a brief time, they reinitiated their surveillance. They found Sparks standing on the side of the road when a dark sedan abruptly pulled up next to him with a white female driver. Sparks jumped into the passenger seat, and the vehicle drove away, but not before Devin took a photo of the license plate.

Ella turned to Devin, seeing the worried look on his face, and realized that this was not just a game anymore. "DJ, what's going on here?"

Devin stood there, not knowing what to think. His gut told him that he'd been betrayed by his friend, but he knew the worst thing he could do was to jump to any unfounded conclusions. He responded to Ella as best he could. "I don't know what's going on, but it doesn't feel right to me. I think we need some help with this one."

The two walked back to the airbase, contemplating their next steps.

While the agents were working inside the detachment the following morning, Devin waited until Sparks left the office to brief Zach on his concerns. "Hey, Zach, man, I know this sounds crazy, but remember what we talked about before, regarding Al?"

"Yeah, what's up?"

"Me and El saw him after work yesterday. For some reason, he was doing a counter-surveillance route in the fish market," Devin explained.

Zach laughed. "What! Ha! Who was chasing him? Wait, what were you two doing in the fish market?"

Ella jumped in. "That's a good question, but that's the wrong question. The right question is, who is that woman he drove away with?"

Devin pulled up the photo of the car. "Yeah, he jumped in some lady's car and drove off. I took this photo and asked Detective Kim to run the tag number. It came back to a Ukrainian diplomat working out of Seoul."

Zach sat there, confused. "What's Al got going on with the Ukrainian embassy?"

"Wait, hold up," said Devin. He vaguely recalled some information that might be helpful. He searched through his notebook and found his notes from the young Security Forces airman. "Remember that SF guy who came in here a few days ago? He was in trouble with his first sergeant for getting married to a juicy girl who's actually Ukrainian and had him send his passport and birth certificate to the Ukrainian embassy to sponsor her pretend brother into South Korea. Both then disappeared."

"Yeah, I remember." The seriousness began to weigh on Zach. "Bro, you don't think Al's gotten mixed up in something like that, do you?"

Devin paused. "I didn't believe you yesterday, but I saw it with my own eyes. Something's going on, and we need to find out before this thing blows up."

"Agreed! So what's the plan?" Zach asked.

Ella sat there quietly, unsure of what to think about Sparks's actions or the steps the agents were about to take to uncover the truth.

"Hey guys, there's something else," Ella whispered. She walked over to retrieve a folded document from her desk. "A few days ago, I was using the copier, and when I was going through my printouts, I noticed I had picked up this document that was still sitting on the machine." Ella handed the paper to Zach with a worried look on her face. "It's Al's birth certificate," she said.

Devin didn't immediately make the connection. "Why was he making copies of his birth certificate, and why is that a big deal?"

Zach folded the document and handed it back to Ella. "Because if he's giving copies of his birth certificate to that Ukrainian woman you saw him with yesterday, we might have a huge problem on our hands."

Devin took a second to absorb the urgency of the situation. "So, either Al is working with the Ukrainians willingly or they have something on him. Is that what you're saying, Zach? Is that what you're telling me?"

"Bro, I don't know what's going on, but when you take his recent behavior, and who he's meeting with, I don't think we have any other choice than to report him to Mullins and Chang as an insider threat," Zach said.

Ella continued to sit quietly as Devin searched for another way to handle the situation. Just then, Detective Kim returned to the office. Devin got an idea.

"Hey, yo, Kim, you still got access to the box?"

Zach couldn't believe that Devin had reached so far so quickly. "The box? Come on, DJ, that's a bit much. Al's supposed to be your boy!"

"He is, and that's the only reason I'm doing this. The only other option is to report him."

Ella stood and walked over to Devin. "DJ, man, you know I love ya, but this is too far."

Detective Kim was unsure of the reason they were asking for her help, but she knew it had to be serious. "If you want it, let me know."

Ella, Zach, and Detective Kim walked away from the bullpen, leaving Devin standing there with a concerned look on his face. He couldn't help but notice his reflection in the mirror—the same mirror that Ella had posed in front of while pretending to be an agent—now held the reflection of someone who wished they were anything but that.

Devin, Ella, and Zach waited inside the hallway of their on-base apartment building. No one spoke, but they all were internally searching for a way to handle the situation without having to brief Agent Chang about Sparks's behavior. Silence filled the corridor as no alternative solutions emerged. The elevator pinged, and the door slid open. Sparks exited, looking down at his phone, unaware of his friends until he was just a few feet away. Still oblivious to the situation, he greeted them with a casual, "What's up, y'all?"

Ella quickly responded, "What's up, Al? You feeling better?"

Sparks had momentarily forgotten the excuse he had given earlier. "What? Oh, yeah, I just needed to step out for a few minutes to get some air. But I'm feeling better now."

"So, you been resting up all day?" Zachary asked.

"Yeah, pretty much. I went for a quick walk earlier, but other than that, I've just been kicking it in my apartment," Sparks replied.

Zach glanced at Devin, who was leaning against the wall, and gave him a nod. Devin looked down at the floor, then forced himself to raise his head and speak to Sparks. "Hey, Al, I got something I wanna show you. Come check this out."

Devin unlocked the door to his apartment and led the others inside. As Sparks entered, he saw Detective Kim sitting at the dining room table, with a fully assembled polygraph machine. All the other chairs had been removed from the dining room, except for one. Bewildered, Sparks asked, "What's all this shit?"

Devin patted him on the shoulder and tried to keep him calm. "Aye, bruh, we've all been cool for a minute, but something ain't adding up."

"Huh, what do you mean?" Sparks responded, trying to keep his voice steady.

Devin looked around the room for support, then asked Sparks, "Where did you go yesterday?"

Still trying to control his emotions, Sparks began gesturing with his hands. "I already told y'all. I didn't go nowhere."

Zach walked over and sat down on the table. "So who was that Ukrainian woman driving the car you left in?"

Realizing he had been followed, Sparks became enraged. He slowly turned to Ella, shook his head in disappointment, and then looked at Devin as if he had been betrayed by his best friends. "That was nothing. I don't know what you're talking about."

Zach pressed harder. "If you don't tell us, you can explain your secrecy to Agent Mullins."

Sparks threw his keys down on the table. "Damn you and Mullins. I'm not doing this stupid shit! Move out the way!" Sparks realized that in his anger, his fists had balled up, so he grabbed his keys and turned to walk out the door. Devin stepped in front of him, putting a hand on Sparks's chest to stop him. Sparks pushed Devin over the table, knocking several items onto the floor.

Ella screamed and yelled, "Stop! Stop! Y'all are friends!"

Zach quickly restrained Sparks from assaulting Devin, who was on the floor. Devin stood up, stepped in front of Sparks, then moved aside to allow him to exit the apartment. Devin reached into his pocket and pulled out Sparks's birth certificate. Sparks looked down at the document and snatched it from Devin's hand.

Suddenly regretting what had just happened, Sparks said, "Look, I can't—I can't say. I would, but I can't."

"Sorry, Al, that's just not good enough," Zach said calmly as he sat back down on the table.

Sparks stared at the door but knew that leaving would only make things worse. Against his better judgment, he began to explain his behavior to the team. "Alright, look, I was working a joint UC op with the Agency."

"You were undercover?" Ella asked.

"Yeah. The Agency sent Agent Chang a heads-up that the Ukrainians were gathering intel from service members. They found a threat from a foreign intelligence service operating at a hotel in Busan. My job was to meet her, make her comfortable, and feed her bad intel."

Devin squinted, trying to read Sparks's body language. "Is that the truth?"

Sparks nodded. "Yes. They didn't even tell Mullins because her husband is from the Ukraine, and they didn't want to create a conflict of interest. So she never knew what was going on."

"What about the birth certificate?" Zach asked.

Sparks clearly didn't want to discuss the document. "It has nothing to do with any of this. I've got some personal stuff going on back home."

Devin listened to Sparks's answer and walked around the table to stand behind Detective Kim. "If that's the truth, then you won't mind letting Kim check you out, right?"

Once again, Sparks became outraged, but this time, instead of breaking things, he sat down next to Detective Kim and held his arm out for her to hook up the polygraph leads. "When this is done, I'm whooping all y'all asses."

Once the wires were connected, Detective Kim began asking basic questions to establish a baseline. Devin, Zach, and Ella stood in the back of the room, watching from a short distance. Devin, still uncertain whether his actions were right, kept staring at the floor, finding it difficult to watch Sparks being humiliated. Ella seemed very intrigued by the process, losing herself in the drama as though she were watching a movie.

A few minutes later, Detective Kim took off her glasses and

sat back in her chair. "Am I done yet?" Sparks asked.

"Yes, the test is complete," Detective Kim replied, "And he's squeaky clean."

Upon hearing that, Sparks stood up and began ripping the wires from his arm. With his hands in his pockets, Devin slowly walked over to Sparks. "You know this was Zach's idea, right? I didn't believe a word he said. Now he got you in here all wired up like a Cyborg! We good, bruh?" Devin extended his hand, hoping that Sparks would return the gesture.

After a short pause, Sparks looked around the room and smiled. "Yeah, we're good. Man, I was getting tired of holding that secret anyway. And Ella, you did a decent job with your surveillance. I had no idea you were trailing me."

The team laughed together as Detective Kim stood up to disassemble her machine. "Well, hey, since we got all this equipment out here, who wants to go next?" Ella joked.

Sparks pushed her down in the seat. "Looks like you're going next!"

Detective Kim quickly hooked the leads up to Ella and the team took turns asking her simple questions. Devin asked if she enjoyed her assignment with OSI. Ella replied, "Yes," and Detective Kim nodded to show she was truthful. Seeing an opportunity to lighten the mood, Sparks asked the next question. "Do you really buy your clothes at the thrift store?"

"That's an easy one. Yes," Ella said, resulting in another positive nod from Detective Kim.

Although Devin and Sparks understood to only ask

lighthearted questions, Zach was determined to use the situation to find out information that had been eluding him for weeks. He walked over to Ella, looked into her eyes, and asked, "Do you have a secret romance with DJ?"

Ella was stunned and looked directly at Devin, whose mouth dropped as he tried to stop her from answering. "No!" Ella responded. Silence filled the room as everyone waited for Detective Kim's determination. Not wanting to embarrass Ella, she turned her head and quietly stated, "Deception detected."

"I knew it!" Zach yelled.

Sparks was confused. "What? When did this happen?"

Devin didn't say a word; he just turned and walked out of the apartment. Ella called for him as he walked out the door. Sparks laughed. "Don't worry, he'll be back. This is his apartment."

The next day, things seemed to be back to normal inside the detachment. The agents were working on their individual cases, and Ella was conducting an audit of the contingency funds. Agent Chang walked back to the bullpen with an excited look on his face. "Hey, guys, we got it! We got the taxi! The owner is going to drop it off at 2200 hours and allow us to search it."

The agents slowly turned to look at each other. "Ten o'clock, tonight?" Sparks asked.

"Yeah, tonight," Chang replied. "Dress warm; this should be fun."

The agents were excited to get their hands on the vehicle, but it was late January in South Korea, meaning it would be extremely cold during their search. Later that night, the agents took possession of the vehicle and parked it inside an empty aircraft hangar. Even with the hangar doors closed, the temperature was barely out of the single digits. The agents did their best to dress for the event, but it didn't help. Agent Sparks wore a large parka with thick gloves that made handling any equipment difficult. Devin had a black ski mask, with nothing visible on his face except his eyes and mouth. They had also requested the help of the base photographer to document the scene. When they were ready to begin, they opened all four doors of the car and sprayed the interior with luminol to detect any bodily fluids that might still be present from Wilson's ride to his apartment. They extinguished the hangar lights and turned on the ultraviolet wand. The entire inside of the taxi began to glow with a fluorescent green hue. The chemical had detected multiple types of body fluid all over the taxi. Everyone stood in silence, amazed at what they were viewing.

"That's the most disgusting shit I've ever seen in my life!" Sparks exclaimed.

Zach, who was already a closeted germophobe, wasn't sure how to react. He was thrilled to be processing the crime scene, but the thought of touching anything in that car made him question his dedication to the job. "I'm never riding in a taxi again for the rest of my life," Zach mumbled as he grabbed the fluorescent light and began to inspect the back seat. Although thoroughly repulsed, Zach still managed to conduct an extremely thorough examination and found what appeared to be a drop of blood on the interior right rear door panel. They placed a small amount in a test kit, and the results were positive. However, they couldn't rely on their field kit alone, so they carefully removed the specimen and packaged it for examination by USACIL.

Within about two hours, the examination was completed. Sparks asked Devin to ride with him as he drove the photographer back to the base command post. Devin agreed and hopped into the front passenger seat. By this time, it was a few minutes after midnight. As they drove across the base, Devin noticed a lone vehicle sitting in the parking lot of the Shoppette. As they got closer, he noticed an older Korean lady, dressed in a long coat, gloves, and a scarf, loading groceries into her car. Devin became suspicious because the Shoppette had been closed for two hours. He asked Sparks to pull the vehicle behind the woman. As the vehicle slowed to a halt, Devin rolled down the window and yelled at the woman to get her attention.

"Hey! Hey! What are you doing? Hey!"

The woman turned around, saw Devin, and completely freaked out. She slammed her trunk shut and ran around to the driver's side door. Devin stepped out of his car and attempted to stop the woman before she drove off, but he was called back by Sparks.

"Dude, dude, take off your ski mask!"

Devin stood there, confused as to why Sparks had helped the woman get away from him. "Take off what, my mask? Oh, snap!" Devin turned to watch the woman drive out of the parking lot and wondered what she had been thinking when a Black man wearing a ski mask at midnight started yelling at her and chased her back to her vehicle. He got back into the car, and the three men laughed for the next five minutes before dropping off the photographer.

Since they worked until around one o'clock in the morning, the agents didn't report to work until after lunch the following day. Everyone was optimistic about the blood Zach had found inside the taxi, and they all agreed on the next course of action: they would administer polygraph tests to both Wilson and Ramirez. Unfortunately, they needed to wait a few weeks for the blood sample to be examined by USACIL. While they waited for the results, the agents took turns reviewing the daily videos captured by the tech agents and logging pertinent evidence into the case file. Although they weren't actively working on the Brunelle assault case, they had several other investigations that kept them busy, along with military exercises.

CHAPTER 7
COCAINE COWBOYS

A few days later

Agent Sparks traveled to the Medical Group at the request of one of his open contacts, Captain Jaqueline Walters, who oversaw the ADAPT (Alcohol and Drug Abuse Prevention and Treatment) program at Osan. The program was designed to give second chances to airmen who self-identified as substance abuse users. Sparks arrived at the ADAPT office, and Capt. Walters quickly ushered him into her office.

"Al, thanks for stopping by. Look, I won't hold you, but there's something you need to be aware of. Senior Airman Gary Simmons has been treated here multiple times, and we believe he committed identity theft."

"Identity theft? Why do you think that?"

"When our members attend meetings here, they're required to sign in on the attendance sheet with their name and social security number so that we can enter their treatment into their medical records."

"Yeah, that's probably not smart—having their socials out in the open like that. How do you know he stole their identities?"

"Several of our members have come back to us complaining that they've received fraud alerts from their banks. Some of them discovered that credit accounts had been fraudulently opened in their names. At first, I had no idea it was happening here in our office, but I started watching the sign-in sheet more closely. During the last two meetings, I saw Airman Simmons sign in with his cell phone in his hand, and he appeared to have taken a photo of the attendance log."

"Yep, that'll do it. Where is he now? Is he part of the Medical Group?"

"No, he works at the Civil Engineering Squadron."

Sparks requested a list of potential victims. Capt. Walters handed the list to Sparks, and the two stood in awkward silence for a couple of seconds. Sparks and Walters had become friends over the previous months and had hung out a few times. Even though there was obvious chemistry between them, Capt. Walters was hesitant to pursue it because she was an officer and Sparks was an NCO. She didn't want to risk her career over fraternization, though she had come close to doing so on multiple occasions. Sparks offered a quick hug and left the office.

Sparks returned to the detachment and, after briefing Agent Mullins, initiated a fraud investigation into the stolen identities. Over the next few days, he interviewed six airmen who claimed to have had their identities stolen and verified they were all under treatment at the ADAPT center. While he was at his desk typing up the interviews, the detachment received a BOLO from Security Forces stating that Senior Airman Gary Simmons had gone AWOL. Sparks was eager to kick off a search for Simmons but was reminded by Mullins that they couldn't do anything until he had been AWOL for thirty days. So, Sparks continued pressing forward with his fraud case.

Three weeks later, in mid-February, Colonel Urquidez, Agent Chang's boss and the commander of the OSI Squadron overseeing all the OSI Detachments in Korea, walked from his office across the parking lot and into the detachment. He told Agent Chang that he had some exciting news and to gather the team for a quick meeting. Once the team had assembled in the conference room, Colonel Urquidez jumped to his feet, barely able to contain his excitement. The agents were eager to hear his announcement.

"Good afternoon, everyone. I know you're all busy, but I've got some great news to share. Starting next week, we'll be formally participating in the Wing's war exercise! So, get your chem suits ready! Staff Sergeant Arnold will be working with the Command Post and Security Forces to generate a few exercises for us. And, on top of that, I've volunteered our team to serve as OPFOR against the Security Forces Forward Operating Base. It should be a fun time, and I know you all will make me proud."

None of the agents were pleased with this news. They had managed to evade the last two exercises due to real-world investigations demanding their attention. However, with the current lull in operations, the team couldn't avoid this round of drills. They complained to Chang and Mullins that their workload was too heavy to pause, but there was nothing Chang could do since the direction came directly from his boss. Mullins only reminded them that their deadlines wouldn't be extended, even though they wouldn't be allowed to do any case work during the exercise.

On the first day of the exercise, the agents began their day as usual, battling the ever-growing mounds of paperwork. A sense of dread hung in the office as they all knew the "fun" was about to start. Then they heard it—the alarm went off, and the entire base went into MOPP 2. They struggled to don their chem suits and headed to the storage room, now designated as the command center. For some reason, the room was decked out in camouflage, and they all wondered who had found the time to put up the decorations. Devin, Sparks, Zach, and Ella sat anxiously in the command center for two hours, staring at each other. They were working mandatory twelve-hour shifts and began to wonder if the entire exercise would consist of walking back and forth inside their compound.

Suddenly, a call came over the radio. "Shadow One, Raven One." Everyone stared at the radio as if it were a piece of talking furniture. "Shadow One, Raven One." The team looked at each other as though the person on the radio was speaking a foreign language.

"Who the hell is Shadow One?" Sparks asked.

Zach shrugged. "Are they supposed to be calling us?"

Ella, who would normally have turned the situation into a comedy, was frustrated with the team's lack of preparation for the exercise. She shook her head and leaned over to Devin, who was also clueless about the radio. "Devin, you need to answer the radio. Shadow One is the call sign for OSI. You are Shadow One."

"Shit!" Devin jumped up too quickly, tripped over the thick rubber boots he was wearing as part of his chem suit, and fell against the table, breaking one of its legs and knocking the entire radio set and the exercise notes onto the floor. Sparks and Zach erupted in laughter. Ella, embarrassed for Devin, suppressed her laughter to avoid making him feel any worse. While sitting on the floor, Devin picked up the radio and keyed the mic. "Raven One, Shadow One."

There was a brief silence, then a response: "Yeah, hey, Shadow One. Just doing a radio check. How copy?"

Still sitting on the floor, ashamed of his mishap over a simple radio check, Devin responded, "Lima, Charlie. Shadow One, out!"

The next day started out more eventfully as the agents spent the morning responding to suspicious items and conducting mock interviews with role players pretending to plot a terrorist attack. The agents tried to remain upbeat because they knew what was planned for the afternoon: Colonel Urquidez's attack on the

Security Forces compound. At 1700 hours, the agents geared up with their modified M-4 rifles and split into two teams. Colonel Urquidez briefed them on the attack plan, using a crayon-drawn mock compound on the table.

"The compound is located way on the backside of the runway, near the farms. We'll break into two teams. We're going to have to approach on foot from the runway, or else they'll see us coming. Sparks, you come with me. The rest of you go with Agent Chang and attack the compound from the front."

The team set off, and ten minutes later, Devin, Zach, and Chang were trudging through two feet of snow, trying to surprise the guards manning the compound.

"Hey guys, we gotta get lower—get down, or they'll see us," Chang said.

The team low-crawled through the snow for the next quarter mile. By the time they got close to the compound, it was dark, but before they could initiate any time of assault, Security Forces launched multiple flares and spotted them immediately. The fight was on—and over just as fast. Devin didn't even get a chance to fire his rifle. Humiliated but relieved to be getting out of the cold, the team returned to their compound. They expected to see Sparks when they arrived, as they hadn't seen any sign of him or Colonel Urquidez out on the field.

Forty-five minutes later, as the team was explaining to Ella how badly they had failed on the battlefield, the compound door flew open, and in walked Agent Sparks, dripping wet and mad as hell.

"Al, what happened bro?" Zach asked.

"What you mean, what happened? Man, look at my clothes—it's fifteen degrees outside, and this crazy heifer wanted to go swimming!" Sparks fumed.

No one knew what to say as Sparks marched over to one of the tables to unload his gear. He walked past Ella, who had a strange look on her face, as though something smelled ... foul.

"You wanna tell us what happened there, stinky?" Ella joked.

"We were walking through the snow, a little bit north of where you guys were. Then we came up on a stream—it was about fifteen feet wide, but the water had snow and ice on top of it, so we couldn't tell how deep it was. I found a stick and stuck it in the stream; and it was about two feet deep beside the bank. So, I pulled the stick out and told him we needed to backtrack and find another way to the compound. But this crazy dude jumps into the stream and tells me to hurry up and get in! I should have known not to get in that damn water! Man, I jumped in, and we started making our way across, and I noticed the water didn't smell right. Then the Colonel tells me they use the stream as a runoff from the farms and it's full of cow manure. Now I'm halfway across the stream, and it drops to about four feet. I'm up to my waist in shit water, and my boot got caught on something at the bottom of the stream."

Ella covered her eyes, bracing herself for Sparks to say that he had stuck his head under the water.

"As I'm trying my best to pull my foot from the snag, the Colonel says, 'Hey, you might want to hurry up!' I turned around, and there was a dead cow floating down the stream, coming right at me. So, I turned my back to the cow and started pulling as hard as I could."

"What? Where was the Colonel?" Zach asked.

"His ass was standing on the other side of the creek, laughing!" Sparks shouted, as Agent Chang turned his head and pretended not to hear anything Sparks had said. Soon after that, the night shift arrived, and the agents headed home.

The next day, the agents dragged themselves back into the command post and awaited the next emergency call. To their surprise, Agent Chang walked in with good news.

"Hey, guys, the Colonel was really happy with the effort you put in last night and has decided to pull you out of the remainder of the exercise. You can go back to work now."

Feeling exonerated, the agents and Ella quickly discarded their MOPP gear and made their way back to the detachment. Not long after getting settled, Agent Mullins stepped into the bullpen.

"Hey, guys, just got a call from the Law Enforcement desk—they found a dead body in the dorms. I need two of you to respond to the scene."

The agents all seemed to have the same question. "Is this real-world or part of the exercise?" Sparks asked.

Realizing she hadn't verified whether it was a real emergency, Mullins stood there with a guilty look on her face. "Just go check it out and let me know," she said, as she turned and walked back to her office.

Five minutes later, Devin and Zach arrived at the dormitory. They weren't sure exactly where the crime scene was, but as soon as they opened the door on the first floor, they saw Security Forces guards, the First Sergeant, and the Squadron Commander standing over a body that was face down on the floor. They showed their credentials to the guards, who allowed them to enter the area. As they approached, the First Sergeant and Commander walked up to them and began rattling off information about how they found the body, what they thought happened, and who had been in the area. Since the body was face down, the agents couldn't see any obvious injuries. The First Sergeant and Commander stared at the agents, waiting for them to respond.

After staring at the body for a moment, Devin turned to the Commander. "Is this a real dead body, or are y'all just playing?"

The Commander looked thoroughly confused. "This is an exercise event. You guys were supposed to respond and process the crime scene."

The agents, still tired from the previous day, showed no interest in playing along. "Yeah, we're not doing that," Devin said as he and Zach turned and walked back down the hallway. The Security Forces guards giggled as the agents walked by, leaving the Squadron Commander standing there, unsure of what to do.

When Devin and Zach arrived back at the office, Agent Mullins was on a call with the Commander, apologizing that the agents had left the scene because they "had more important things to do." When Mullins finished the call, she walked back to the bullpen and approached Devin. "Hey, I need you to follow up with the counterintelligence team about suspicious calls going to the elementary school." She then turned and walked back to her office without mentioning what had happened at the dormitory.

The next morning, Sparks and Zach were having breakfast off-base, laughing about their experiences during the exercise. By this time, Zach had spent so much time around Sparks and Devin that their style had begun to rub off on him. Zach had started wearing clothes that were a bit looser, and his beard was now thicker than Sparks's. As they were eating, Sparks noticed someone across the restaurant who looked familiar. He kept glancing over at the young man, who was oblivious to his surroundings as he played games on his cell phone.

"That's ol' boy!" Sparks exclaimed.

"Who's ol' boy?" Zach asked.

"That's the guy who went AWOL last month."

As Zach turned to catch a glimpse, the man stood up and walked out of the restaurant. The agents quickly finished their breakfast and returned to the office to brief Agent Mullins. They were shocked to learn that the thirty days had expired, and they were now authorized to track down Airman Simmons. As Sparks and Zach sat in the office brainstorming ways to find Simmons, Devin walked in on their conversation and shared his idea.

"Why don't you guys ask Samantha if she knows him?"

"Who's Samantha," Sparks asked.

"Zach's juicy girl informant. Maybe she's seen him in the clubs," Devin replied.

Zach was hesitant to get her involved but ultimately agreed to ask for her assistance.

Later that night, Sparks and Zach went to Samantha's bar and found her dancing on stage in a bikini. She spotted Zach and ran over to hug him. "Hey Zach, I'm happy to see you. What's going on?"

Zach introduced Samantha to Sparks as he pulled a photo of Simmons out of his coat pocket. "Hey, I know it's a long shot, but it's really important that we find this guy. Have you seen him?"

Samantha stared at the photo for a couple of seconds. "Yeah, I think so," she replied. "He's been in here a few times, but I never talk to him. He usually asks for Amy when he's here."

Sparks interjected. "Great. Is Amy here, and can we speak to her?"

"Yeah, hold on a minute," Samantha said as she walked over to the Ajeema sitting at the bar. She returned with a concerned look on her face. "Ajeema says you can talk to Amy, but you have to buy us both drinks first."

"Yeah, that's not a problem," Sparks said as he motioned for the waitress. About a minute later, Amy joined them at their table. Samantha introduced Zach and Sparks as her friends and told Amy that they needed her help. Sparks discreetly pulled the photo back out of his jacket and showed it to Amy. She looked at the picture, then turned around to see if Ajeema was watching. She said something to Samantha in Tagalog but was ultimately reassured she could trust the agents.

"Yes, I know him," Amy said.

"Do you know where he lives?" Sparks asked.

Amy shook her head. "No, but I know where his wife works."

"His wife? He's married? To who?" Sparks asked.

"Well, she calls him her husband. Her name is Daisy, and she works at the Gold Bar down the street."

"Hold up. I'm confused," Zach said. "Is the guy married or not?"

Samantha intervened, explaining that Simmons must have paid off Daisy's debt to the bar owner, which then allowed Simmons to take her home with him every night.

Sparks and Zach made their way to the bar where Simmons's wife was reported to be working. Knowing they would arouse too much suspicion if they started asking questions directly, they ordered a couple of drinks and began chatting with the waitress. After a few minutes, Sparks casually asked if she knew a bar girl named Daisy. The waitress nodded and pointed out Daisy, who was sitting at the bar talking to a couple of GIs.

Sparks excused himself to use the restroom but instead made his way to the bar. He discreetly showed the two service members his credentials and asked them to leave so he could speak with Daisy. After they left, Sparks introduced himself as an agent and asked Daisy if she was familiar with Airman Simmons. Daisy hesitantly said yes, and Sparks showed her his picture to confirm.

Daisy grew nervous, fearing she was in trouble. She had heard about locals getting into legal issues for black marketing and didn't want to get arrested for abusing Simmons's benefits.

"So, are you guys really married?" Sparks asked.

Daisy replied, "Not really married, but he bought off my bar tab, so I'm free to do whatever I want. I don't have enough money yet to go back home, so I'm still working here. Why are you asking me these questions? Is there some kind of trouble?"

Sparks chuckled. "Yeah, your boy Simmons has gotten himself into a heap of shit!"

"What do you mean?" Daisy asked, her concern growing.

"He's AWOL—absent without leave—and when we catch him, he's going to jail."

Daisy, fearing she might get caught up in Simmons's activities, quickly decided to cooperate fully with the agents. When Sparks asked if she knew where Simmons was at that moment, she said, "Yes, he's at our apartment. I can take you there."

Fifteen minutes later, Sparks and Zach were sitting in a vehicle with Daisy, about a block away from Simmons's apartment. They could see the light from the television through the window. Sparks called back to Mullins and informed her that they had located Simmons. Mullins instructed the agents to stand by while she coordinated with the KNP and the rest of the detachment to assist.

Within an hour, Detective Kim, her KNP unit, and the remaining agents joined Sparks and Zach at their location. After a quick briefing, the KNP stacked up on the door and kicked it in. Sparks quickly entered the apartment and found Airman Simmons sitting in his living room in his underwear, eating a bowl of cereal. He was terrified when the door flew open and he was suddenly surrounded by armed agents.

"Senior Airman Simmons, I'm Special Agent Al Sparks, OSI. We're taking you into custody for being AWOL. Get your dumb ass up and let's go!"

The following morning, Devin received a call at his desk from the counterintelligence team. He grabbed Sparks's attention, and the two went to brief Agent Mullins.

"Hey, you know that incident we spoke about regarding the suspicious calls at the elementary school? Turns out, someone kept calling the classroom, and one of the kids answered the phone. The caller started asking if this was an Air Force base and if the child could see any airplanes from where she was. It seemed like a CI issue at first, but it turns out it was Korean Customs Enforcement calling. They intercepted a package mailed from Texas, addressed to the schoolteacher. Their K-9 unit hit on the package, so they opened it and found cocaine inside. They're planning to have the teacher take possession of the package and then arrest him. They want us to go with them. It's all happening at his apartment downtown," Devin said.

Mullins agreed that the agents should be involved since the teacher was employed at Osan, so the agents left and met with six Customs Enforcement officers a few blocks away from the teacher's apartment building.

When Devin and Sparks arrived, Detective Kim was already on the scene and introduced them to the Customs officers. They explained that after finding the cocaine, they resealed the box and arranged for a delivery service to drop off the package. As soon as the teacher signed for it, they would make the arrest. One of the officers pulled the package out of a plastic bag, and the agents burst into laughter. The officers had tried to reseal the small brown box with gray duct tape, making it look like a five-year-old had attempted to rewrap his Christmas presents.

Just then, the delivery service arrived on a motorcycle. They explained the situation to the driver, who took one look at the package and drove away, leaving the officers on the side of the road holding a box of cocaine. At that moment, Devin and Sparks agreed to step back and just observe the operation, as all signs were pointing toward potential disaster. And they were right.

The Customs officers drove over to the apartment complex and walked into the security office, located about thirty yards from the building. They instructed the security guard to call the teacher down to the office to retrieve his package. The guard agreed, phoned the teacher's apartment, and told him to come downstairs to sign for it. The agents could hear the teacher's response over the phone: "What package? I'm not expecting any packages. I'm not coming down there!" The teacher hung up.

The Customs officers became upset and pressured the security guard to call again, insisting the teacher come down. Once again, the teacher denied having a package but said he would come downstairs to examine the box. When the officers realized the teacher was coming down from the third floor, they panicked. They started running around the parking lot, bumping into each other, and nearly fighting over hiding spots. Eventually, they ducked behind a few parked cars and waited for the teacher to arrive.

"Bruh, what kind of foolishness is going on here? I'm not trying to be a part of this shit!" Sparks said.

Devin agreed, and after witnessing the chaos, the agents decided to walk back to their vehicle on the other side of the parking lot and watch the transaction through their rearview mirror.

A few minutes later, the teacher arrived at the security shack. He looked at the package and continued to insist that it wasn't his. The security guard, nervous about what the Customs officers might say to him, practically forced the teacher to take the package back to his apartment. Once the teacher had returned to his home, the Customs officers reappeared and quickly devised a plan to enter his home and arrest him for possession. They requested the agents' assistance in the arrest, but Devin and Sparks wanted no parts of the operation. They agreed to watch from the fourth-floor balcony as the Customs officers attempted the arrest on the third floor.

After about fifteen minutes, the Customs officers knocked on the teacher's door. There was no answer. They continued knocking for the next ten minutes. Still no answer. One of the officers went down to the guard shack and had the security guard call the apartment, but no one answered. The Customs officers began to panic, and rightfully so. Devin and Sparks stood back, watching from a distance.

"Bruh, these dudes just lost a whole box of cocaine," Devin joked. "Let's go back to the car."

As soon as they got back to the car, Sparks called Mullins to ensure she knew they had no involvement in losing the drugs. Then they laughed for the next half hour. Finally, Detective Kim called and said the teacher had returned and they needed assistance speaking with him. When the agents arrived at the apartment, the teacher, a mid-forties African American man, ran up to them, pleading for help.

"Can you please tell me what's going on? These dudes busted into my apartment screaming at me in Korean. I don't know what they're talking about!"

Inside, the Customs officers were conducting a search and had ransacked the entire place.

Sparks explained to the teacher that they suspected him of receiving drugs through the mail. The man became irate, insisting the package wasn't his and that the security guard had forced him to take it. He then admitted that sometimes one of his former students had packages sent to the teacher's address. The teacher called the student, who denied expecting a package but agreed to stop by to see if it had come from his family. The student was only five minutes away—cue the shenanigans.

The officers decided to hide inside the apartment, and chaos ensued as they ran around, bumping into each other while looking for hiding places. Once again, Devin and Sparks stood back and laughed as the officers hid behind couches and inside closets, waiting for the student to arrive. The agents returned to their vehicle, only to get a call a few minutes later to come back.

As they approached the door, they noticed that while the officers had hidden inside the apartment, they had left six pairs of shoes at the front door—making it obvious that they were inside. The student had arrived and also denied ownership of the package. Finally realizing they had completely botched the investigation, the officers turned to the agents and asked if they wanted to take possession of the cocaine.

Sparks replied, "Nah, we're good. You guys can go ahead and keep it. We're gonna head on back to the base. Y'all have a good night."

The two agents laughed the entire ride back to Osan, imagining what would have happened to them if they had lost a box of cocaine. Although the operation with the Customs investigators was heavily flawed, it sparked an idea about recruiting another potential source.

The next morning, Devin reviewed his list of attendees from the last Newcomer's Briefing at the First Term Airman's Center and highlighted the name Airman Miranda Patterson, who just started her first assignment at the base post office. Realizing they didn't have any personal contacts there, they called Airman Patterson in for an interview.

When she arrived, the agents put her at ease and explained that they needed her assistance. Since she would likely be one of the first people to notice any suspicious packages arriving on base, they wanted her as one of their contacts. Although Airman Patterson was only eighteen, she displayed a level of maturity during the meeting. She wanted to think about their offer for a few days before signing any paperwork but gave the impression that she would be on board.

CHAPTER 8

THROUGH THE FIRE

A few days later

Devin and Sparks arrived at the office to find Zach sitting at his desk with a long face. "What's going on Zach? Everything alright?" Sparks asked.

"No, it's not. Take a look at this," Zach replied, handing a large manilla envelope to Sparks. The address on the envelope was from the lab at USACIL, and Sparks knew it had to contain the results from the search of the taxi. He scanned through the paperwork until he landed on the final determination: "The sample was tested for DNA, and the results were INCONCLUSIVE."

"What does this even mean? We tested it here; we know it was blood," Sparks said in disbelief as he handed the paperwork to Devin to review.

"Yeah, that's why I've been sitting here for the last half hour trying to figure out what happened. The only thing I can think of is that when we sprayed the taxi with luminol, the entire car lit up. Since we didn't get the car until several days after the attack, the blood must have been contaminated with every other fluid in that car," Zach said.

A few minutes later, the team met in the conference room with the JAG to brief the status of the case. After hearing that they couldn't rely on the evidence from the taxi, Agent Mullins suggested having Wilson and Ramirez submit to a polygraph. Since the only witness was still in a coma, the polygraph appeared to be the only option.

It took a few days for the agents to prepare for the exam by reviewing all the available evidence and comparing their notes to build a strong interrogation plan. Two hours before the test was to begin, the agents grew anxious and repeatedly reviewed the plan with Detective Kim, who would be administering the test since the crime had occurred off-base. Finally feeling confident about the interview, the agents began to relax, and the mood in the office lightened. Just then, the phone rang at Devin's desk. He recognized the number as belonging to Capt. Murphy from the JAG office. He quickly answered, expecting Capt. Murphy to wish him luck on the interview, but instead received news he never would have expected.

"Hey, Agent Jackson, this is Capt. Murphy. Are you guys still doing the interview today for the assault case?"

"Yeah, the first subject should be here in an hour, and the second guy comes in later this afternoon."

"Oh, okay … um, what were their names again?"

Devin was thrown off, given that they had been briefing JAG on the investigation every week since the case was initiated.

"Tech Sergeant Wilson and Staff Sergeant Ramirez."

"Ahh … I see. I think … I think I may have caused a situation."

"A situation? What's going on? Is everything alright?"

Zach and Sparks both noticed Devin's concern. Then they witnessed his reaction to Capt. Murphy's announcement.

"You did what? What? You did what? Why would you do that?"

Devin listened to the call for a few more seconds and then slammed the phone down. He slowly turned around and sat down on top of his desk. Zach and Sparks couldn't believe the newest development in the case.

"DJ, what happened, man?" Sparks asked.

Devin's blood pressure was shooting sky high as he tried to calm himself enough to explain the situation. "Your JAG officer, you know, Capt. Murphy, the prosecutor on our case, just told Ramirez to ask for an attorney!"

"She did what?" Zach shouted, throwing his case file down onto his desk. Initially, Sparks thought Devin was playing a prank. "Nah, man, she didn't do that. Come on, man."

"Negro! Would I make this shit up?" Devin yelled. "Apparently, she 'forgot' that he was the subject of our case and thought he was just calling for legal advice."

Mullins heard the commotion and walked in to witness the anger emanating from their faces. After being briefed on what happened, Mullins attempted to help the agents regain their composure. "Look, guys, there's nothing we can do about it now. What's done is done. Keep pressing forward with the interview, and if he lawyers up, he lawyers up. That's not on you. I'll have a talk with the boss about Capt. Murphy."

While the agents were still stewing in the bullpen, the Medical Group First Sergeant arrived with Wilson. Zach met him at the door and escorted him to the interview room where Detective Kim was waiting with the polygraph. It took a few minutes to get Wilson hooked up to the machine and past the rights advisement before Detective Kim began asking the questions Zach had prepared regarding the attempted murder of Capt. Brunelle. After the initial baseline questions, Detective Kim signaled to Zach that she was ready to proceed with questioning Wilson.

"Did you meet with Capt. Brunelle on the night he was assaulted?"

"Yes, we hung out at a bar." No deception was detected.

"Did you assault Capt. Brunelle?"

"No, I didn't assault him." No deception was detected.

"Do you know what happened to Capt. Brunelle?"

"No, I don't know what happened to Capt. Brunelle." Results inconclusive.

Detective Kim continued questioning Wilson, but he passed every question except the one that was inconclusive—whether he knew what happened to Capt. Brunelle. Detective Kim finished her interview, and Wilson was released. Thirty minutes later, Ramirez was escorted to the detachment for his turn on the box. Ramirez walked in with an arrogant smirk on his face, as if he already knew the answers to the test. This time, Devin took lead on the interview. He pulled out his rights advisement card and began reading. As soon as Devin announced that Ramirez was suspected of attempted murder, Ramirez interrupted.

"What? Ha! Yo, this guy's crazy, man. I ain't try to kill nobody, man. What's really going on, Special Agent Devin Jackson? Huh? I know you, man. I've seen you downtown … and I know your people." Ramirez slowly tilted his head, trying to read Devin's reaction.

Devin was irritated but tried to remain calm in his best attempt to get Ramirez through the rights advisement. He returned to his card and continued reading. Ramirez's laughter grew louder.

"What do you think happened, Jackson? Huh? And what happened to Wilson? Did he laugh at your dumb ass, too?" Ramirez could see that Devin was flustered. He leaned forward in his chair and whispered, "I want a lawyer." Then he sat back in his seat and looked up at the camera. "Did y'all hear that in the back? I said I want a lawyer!" The interview was over.

After releasing Ramirez, Devin walked back to the bullpen, feeling defeated and was met with words of encouragement from Sparks.

"Damn, man, you let him call you by your government name? I was waiting for you to slap the shit out of that dude."

Devin turned to Sparks and couldn't help but laugh. Soon the whole bullpen was laughing as they realized they had done the best they could. Ella walked over and gave Devin a shoulder hug.

"You good, DJ? What's the plan now?"

No one said a word as they began to face reality: they had no direct evidence, no witnesses, and no confessions.

Ramirez returned to work at the base pharmacy just as the other employees were shutting down for the day. He walked back into Wilson's office, closed the door, and began to question him about his interview.

"What did you tell them?"

"I didn't tell them shit. What did you say?"

"Nothing. I laughed at his dumb ass and asked for a lawyer."

"Who did you have? I had a Korean chick and that red-headed white dude; I can't think of his name."

"Man, I had Jackson. You know, the one that's always hanging out in the clubs with the other Black agent."

"Yeah, I know who you're talking about. I'll tell you what, I'm about tired of these bitches messing up my money. We need to let them know they're not the only ones who can turn up. Know what I'm saying?"

"Nah, what do you mean turn up?"

"I think I know a way you can get even with Jackson, you know, make him back off for a while."

At the same moment, Isabella was walking through the office and overheard Ramirez mention Devin's name. She wasn't sure what he said, but she knew it couldn't be good. She grabbed her purse and headed out of the building. As soon as she cleared the hospital, she pulled out her phone and called Devin's cell. There was no answer, so she left a message:

"Hey, it's Isabella. Look, it's probably nothing, but I was walking by Tech Sgt. Wilson's office and heard him and Ramirez mention your name. Like I said, it's probably nothing, but it seemed weird to me. Okay, call me back sometime. Bye."

Still frustrated from the interviews, Devin left the detachment to blow off some steam and decided to stop by the BX to grab a snack. By this time, it was late afternoon, and the base was bustling with service members shopping and stopping by the BX food court after work. Devin entered the building through the doorway near the post office and turned left to head through the corridor toward the food court.

Suddenly, everyone in the area was startled by the sound of a woman screaming at the top of her lungs. "That's him! That's him! That man's a secret agent! That man right there, he's a secret agent!"

No one, including Devin, knew what the woman was yelling about. He, like everyone else, was confused—until he turned toward the post office and saw Airman Patterson, the young airman he had tried to recruit as an informant a week earlier. She was pointing at him, looking as though she was on the verge of a nervous breakdown.

"That's that man! He's a secret agent! He tried to get me! He's a secret agent!"

At this point, everyone stopped what they were doing and stared at Devin, who just happened to be wearing a black suit with a white shirt. Devin wanted to tell her to "shut up," but he knew it would only make the situation worse, so he kept walking to the food court. As he stood in line, he could feel the eyes on him, people trying to figure out who he was. Needless to say, he took his food to go.

"Why does this crazy stuff keep happening to me?" he muttered to himself.

That Friday night, Ella asked Devin to take her out. She not only wanted to spend time with him, she had noticed how stressed he'd been throughout the week. Around 2100 hours, they left the back gate at Osan and held hands as they strolled through the entertainment district. After an extremely challenging week, this was exactly what Devin needed. They laughed together, relieved that they no longer felt pressured to hide their feelings for each other. Ella made Devin forget about everything except the smile on her face. He had pledged to make her his priority; unfortunately, his focus on her caused him to lose his usual hypersensitivity to his surroundings.

As they walked through the district, Wilson and Ramirez were watching them from a balcony in a restaurant on the other side of the main strip. As the couple passed, Wilson scowled and whispered something to Ramirez.

When Devin and Ella reached the club, they made their way through the crowd and found an empty table across from a couple sitting on a couch. When their drinks arrived, they shared a toast, and Devin pulled Ella close, wrapping his left arm around her as people danced and walked past. Thinking her drink was too strong, Ella took a sip of Devin's to compare the taste.

Wilson entered the nightclub, moving slowly as he pushed through the crowd, appearing to be looking for someone.

Ella leaned over to Devin. "Babe, I'm thinking about cutting my braids off and getting a short hairstyle. What do you think?"

"Hey, anything to make your forehead look smaller."

Ella playfully punched him in the arm, laughing at his joke. While scanning the crowd, she noticed Wilson staring at them. "Hey, DJ, your boy is here, and he's staring at us."

Devin thought Ella was referring to Sparks, so he turned around with a smile, ready to greet his friend. Instead, he found Wilson standing about ten feet away, glaring at him with an intense expression. Devin immediately switched back to "agent mode," locking eyes with the subject of his attempted murder investigation. He remembered that he didn't have his weapon on him, but he wasn't about to let Wilson ruin his night with Ella.

"You good, bruh?" Devin asked as he faced his adversary.

Wilson leaned around Devin and blew a kiss to Ella. Devin sprang to his feet and began storming toward Wilson. He had taken only a couple of steps when Ella grabbed his right arm.

"DJ, stop!"

Devin, now just three feet away from Wilson, shouted, "Is this what you want?"

"Devin! Stop!" Ella screamed, desperately trying to be heard over the blaring music.

Wilson let out a sinister laugh. "Nah, man, I don't want no trouble. I just wanted your pretty girlfriend to know she's got options. That's all."

Before Devin could step forward, two clubgoers who overheard the conversation stepped between the two men. While Ella pleaded with Devin to return to his seat, Ramirez made his way through the crowd and approached their table. While the couple was distracted by Wilson, Ramirez pulled out a small plastic bag containing a fine white powder. He wasn't sure which glass belonged to Devin, but he saw the lipstick on one glass from when Ella tasted Devin's drink and assumed that glass was hers. So, he poured a little of the substance into the other drink but was bumped by someone walking by and ended up pouring the entire amount into the glass. Ramirez froze. He realized the amount he had poured could be deadly and didn't know what to do. So, he simply vanished into the crowd.

After the standoff with Wilson, Devin and Ella returned to their table. Devin was upset that he had let his emotions potentially ruin their night. Ella grabbed his chin and turned his face toward hers. "Hey, don't worry about that. Let's just try to have a good time. Unless you want to leave, we can leave if you want to."

Devin leaned forward to stand from the couch but saw the look on Ella's face and changed his mind. "Nah, I told you we would have a good time tonight, so let's do that." He grabbed his glass and raised it to make a toast with Ella. The glasses clinked, and Ella took a few sips from her drink, the one without lipstick.

As the party continued, the two sat back on their couch and enjoyed the music. Within about fifteen minutes, Ella noticed she had begun to sweat. She grabbed a napkin from the table and wiped her face and neck, but the sweating wouldn't stop. She began to look concerned, unsure of what was happening to her body. Devin hadn't noticed her distress.

"Hey, DJ, I don't feel too good!"

"What's wrong?"

"I don't know. I don't know. Something's not right!"

"Okay, let's go."

Devin stood up and grabbed Ella's hand to help her stand. As soon as she stood, she immediately doubled over with severe abdominal pain. She screamed as her body hit the table when she fell. Devin leaned over to help but didn't understand what was happening. The crowd noticed and began clearing away from Ella. She screamed louder as the pain intensified.

"El, what's wrong? What is it? What's wrong?"

Ella's legs buckled as she collapsed onto the floor. As she screamed, blood began to fill her mouth. She tried to speak but started choking on her own blood. She managed to clear her throat enough to utter one word, "Devin!" Devin was on the floor next to her, trying to hold her head up so she wouldn't choke. He panicked as the club filled with screams and people hurried to get out of the way. "Somebody call an ambulance. Help! Somebody help!"

Security Forces Town Patrol ran through the door and tried to provide aid to Ella. Devin looked up and saw Wilson staring at him with a menacing smirk on his face. About ten minutes later, the paramedics arrived. They asked what had happened, but Devin had no answer for them. Their primary concern was keeping Ella's airway open as she continued to spit up blood. They lifted her onto a gurney and loaded her into the back of the ambulance. Devin was allowed to accompany her, and while the paramedics continued to work on Ella, he called the detachment superintendent.

Within minutes, the ambulance reached the emergency room at Osan. Devin jumped out as Ella was unloaded and rushed inside. He followed close behind. The medical staff seemed bewildered by what was causing Ella's pain. They thought her appendix might have burst and began ordering multiple tests and scans, but there was no time.

Ella continued to scream in agony as even more blood came from her mouth. Her skin began to turn pale. She turned her head and saw Devin standing there, but he was soon pushed up against the wall by the medical staff. Tears flowed from her eyes as she feared what was about to happen. She reached out for Devin, but he was too far away to grab her hand. The medical staff tried to usher him out of the room, but he continued to resist to remain with his girlfriend. Ella tried to talk to him, but the nurse instructed her not to speak as she prepared to insert a tube down her throat to keep her airway open. Ella grabbed the nurse's hand as the tube was forced down. Devin couldn't stand to see her in so much pain but forced himself not to look away.

The medical staff scrambled to find a solution. Suddenly, her body began to convulse violently. It seemed as though Ella knew she could no longer control her body, so she just stared at Devin as the poison took over.

"Ella hang on. Hang on, El, just hang on."

As tears flowed down her face, her eyes, still fixed on Devin, shifted from fear to comfort as the convulsing stopped. Afraid to ask, Devin didn't speak; he only stared into her eyes as her hand went limp. Detached from reality, he heard nothing as the doctor instructed the medical staff to clear before engaging the defibrillator. The nurse released Ella's hand as her body was shocked multiple times before the doctor made the final call. Still focusing on her eyes, Devin knew she was gone. He forgot how to breathe. A couple of nurses grabbed him and tried to force him to sit down. He pushed them away and hurried back to hover over Ella's body.

"Sir, we're going to clean her up. You can come back in a few minutes," the nurse said as she pulled Ella's arm back onto the gurney. Devin stood frozen. The nurse put her arm around Devin, then reached over with her other hand and closed Ella's eyes. He looked at the nurse, who tried to comfort him, but he couldn't comprehend what had happened. He turned and walked out the door, unsure of what to do.

Sparks was in his apartment watching a football game with Zach when he received a call from Mullins that Ella was in the hospital. Sparks and Zach rushed through the emergency room doors, looking around for someone to direct them to her. Just then, they saw Devin walk out of one of the rooms, covered in blood. Devin walked to the middle of the hallway and stopped; he couldn't take another step. His eyes had become glassy as Sparks and Zach ran up to meet him.

Agent Mullins entered the emergency room and saw the agents' behavior. She walked past them to find a doctor to explain what had happened. She stopped a staff member as they were leaving Ella's room. "Doc, is she gonna be alright?"

The doctor didn't respond; he simply shook his head "no" as he began to walk away.

Detective Kim, who had grown close to Ella, arrived at the emergency room, confused by the situation. She saw the agents' reactions and the blood on Devin's shirt. Zach spotted her and tried to walk over to her, but she pushed past him to find Ella's room. She went inside and a few seconds later let out a loud scream, causing Mullins to cry.

The agents took turns going into the room to say goodbye—except for Devin, who tried to enter but couldn't. The team stayed until Ella's body was moved to the morgue.

Mullins walked up to Devin and put her arm around him. "DJ, I know this is tough, but I need you to come by the detachment tomorrow to give a statement."

Sparks, hearing this, was instantly outraged. "A statement? For what? What? You think he was responsible? Nah, man, he ain't doing that."

Mullins calmly responded, "Look, I understand why you're upset, but this may not be from natural causes. I need to get your statement while your memory is still fresh. Anytime tomorrow will be fine."

Zach and Sparks gave Devin a ride back to his apartment. He immediately showered, changed his clothes, and then sat at the kitchen table for the remainder of the night. The next day, Devin arrived at the detachment and was interviewed by Mullins and Agent Chang while Sparks and Zach watched on the video monitor. Devin managed to get through the interview and provided as much detail as he could, but he still had no understanding of what had happened to Ella.

After the interview, Chang informed the team that the KNP would take lead on the investigation, but they agreed to have the autopsy completed in the US to get Ella's body back to her family as soon as possible. A memorial was planned for the next day, and her body would be flown home immediately following the ceremony.

The next day, at 1100 hours, the base chapel filled with people who knew Ella Mae and others who were there to pay their respects. The agents from Detachment 611 sat in the front row, dressed in their service uniforms. Behind them sat Detective Kim and the rest of the KNP investigators who had worked with OSI. A large photograph of Ella rested on an easel at the front of the chapel, surrounded by a beautiful array of flowers.

After the chaplain spoke, Agent Chang shared words about what a wonderful person Ella was and how she would continue to be with each of them in spirit. Each of the agents grieved in their own way. As the service ended, the agents stood and followed the chaplain down the aisle to exit the church. Devin looked out over the crowd, amazed at how many people had come to show support. He couldn't help but think that some of these were the same people who had laughed at him a few months earlier when he introduced himself in this very chapel. Devin wiped his eyes as they made their way down the aisle. Then someone reached out and grabbed his hand. It was Tori, her face reflecting the pain of watching him mourn. She held his hand just long enough for him to see her, then she let it go.

The team was led through the base by a Security Forces escort, driving past the hospital where Ella's remains had been loaded into the back of a hearse. The hearse fell in line behind the escort, and the convoy made its way to the flight line. Along the route, the streets were lined with service members saluting as the hearse passed by. The convoy arrived at the flight line and parked behind a C-17 Globemaster. The agents exited their vehicles and stood facing the rear of the aircraft. The KNP investigators stood a few feet behind them.

"Flight, ten hut!" The agents snapped to attention as the Honor Guard marched toward the hearse.

"Present arms!" The Honor Guard gently pulled the flag-draped transfer case holding Ella's body from the hearse. Her body was marched past the agents and up the ramp of the C-17, where it was carefully laid on the floor of the cargo bay.

"Order arms!" As the agents dropped their salute, Devin stepped out from the formation and walked up the ramp. He was still in shock, barely aware of how he had gotten dressed that morning, but there he was, saying goodbye. He knelt beside the transfer case and placed his hand on top of the flag.

"I'm sorry, El. I'm sorry. It's all my fault. It's all my fault. I'm sorry."

A few moments passed, and he didn't know how to leave. Then he felt a hand on top of his; Detective Kim had walked inside the airplane to help him say goodbye. The two stood up, Devin gave Kim a quick nod, and they walked back down the ramp. Sparks and Zach, concerned for their friend, watched as he walked past the formation and exited the flight line alone. The transfer case was secured, and the cargo bay doors closed. Twenty minutes later, the agents watched as the aircraft lifted off, carrying Ella's remains home to her family.

Devin walked away from the ceremony and arrived at the empty OSI detachment. He had intended to sit at his desk but was drawn to Ella's. He stared at her photo still sitting at her workstation and then sat in her chair for the next hour until he heard the rest of the team entering the building. Quietly, he returned to his desk and stared at his blank computer screen. Sparks and Zach joined him in the bullpen, and the three of them sat in silence for several hours, well into the night. They couldn't believe that just three days earlier, Ella was sitting with them, making jokes at their expense.

The next few days were a blur. The office was quiet, as no one really knew what to say about the tragedy. There was nothing the agents could do about Ella's death until the toxicology report came back. For all they knew at that time, she might have died of natural causes. Devin stared at his computer screen all day, but no work was getting done. When Devin stepped away from his desk, Zach looked over the divider and saw that Devin had been drawing circles on a notepad the entire day. He was handling things in his own way, and Mullins was in no hurry to put him back into stressful situations.

Toward the end of the week, Devin arrived at the detachment just in time for the morning staff meeting. He entered the building and walked into the conference room as the meeting was about to begin. Normally, Agent Chang would have been upset about someone arriving at the last minute, but instead of badgering Devin about being on time, Chang was actually happy to see him willing to continue working.

The meeting started, and as usual, Chang asked each agent what they had planned for the day. Agent Zachary replied, "I've got the Howard interview today. He's the Staff Sergeant in my rape case—you know, the one where the girl woke up in his dorm room and didn't even know how she got there."

Agent Chang acknowledged and asked Zach if he needed any assistance.

"Actually, yeah," said Zach. "I need a hand with the interrogation—just somebody to take notes for me. Al, can you help me out?"

Agent Sparks politely declined, explaining that he had to complete the evidence review in place of Ella. Devin volunteered to help during the interview, but Zach was hesitant to accept his help.

"You sure, man? I mean, you've got a lot going on right now."

Devin understood Zach's concern. "Zach, I got it, man, I'm good."

A couple of hours later, Zach began his interrogation of Howard about the sexual assault. No matter how hard Zach pushed him, Howard didn't break and consistently repeated his alibi. Devin grew increasingly annoyed, scribbling the same excuses over and over on his notepad. He couldn't understand why Zach hadn't turned up the pressure on Howard as he had in other interrogations.

Zach continued his line of questioning, trying to determine whether the victim was coherent when the assault took place.

"Look, man, she wanted it. She couldn't keep her hands off me!" Howard shouted.

"So why didn't she know where she was when she woke up?" Zach asked.

Howard looked around the room and began chuckling. "I don't know. You gotta ask that bitch! I'm telling you, bro, she wanted it!"

Something about Howard's demeanor triggered Devin. Without thinking, he interrupted the interview. "If you raped her, then just say you raped her. You're playing games right now!"

Caught off guard by the outburst, Zach tried to calm the situation. "DJ, hold on, man." He then continued with his questioning. "Do you know of any witnesses who can corroborate your story?"

Again, Devin disrupted the interrogation. "Nah, man, he raped that girl. Say you raped her! You're strong enough to assault the girl, but you're too scared to admit to what you did. Say you did it! Say you raped her! Say it!"

Howard's confidence wavered, thrown off by Devin's outburst. "Okay, what's going on here?" he asked.

Before Zach could respond, Devin sprang to his feet and stood within inches of Howard's face. "Say that shit!" Devin yelled.

"DJ, I got it," Zach said nervously, feeling he had completely lost control of his own interview. However, Devin seemed oblivious to his surroundings, fixated on whatever had ignited his anger. Zach looked up at the monitor and motioned for Sparks to assist. Seconds later, Sparks opened the door and called Devin into the hallway.

"Alright, man, you're done for the day. I'll finish this up," said Sparks.

The next day was much the same. Devin spoke little and accomplished nothing. Every second was spent thinking of Ella and what could have happened to her that night. The more he dwelled on her, the more depressed he became. This time, there was no one in the office to lift his spirits, as Sparks and Zach were across the base conducting interviews. As he fought back the emotions, the office phone rang. He cleared his throat.

"OSI, Agent Jackson, can I help you?"

"Oh, hey Agent Jackson, this is Sergeant Ramirez from the pharmacy. Listen, I just wanted to call and give my condolences for the young lady who passed away. I don't know what her name was, but it seemed like you two were really close. So, maybe she learned the hard way to pick her friends better. Right?"

"What did you say?"

"Look man, I'm just saying. If you had just minded your business, you know … maybe that bitch would still be alive."

Devin slammed the phone down, grabbed the keys to one of the vehicles, and sped out of the parking lot. Sparks and Zach were on their way back from their interviews and noticed one of their cars speeding down the road.

"Al, wasn't that DJ?" Zach asked.

"Yeah, I think so. Where is he going?" Sparks asked as he pulled onto the road to follow and see where his friend was headed.

Devin sped through the base and abruptly pulled up in front of the hospital. He jumped out of the car and stormed into the building and down the halls until he reached the pharmacy, with no concern for his consequences. He tried to open the side door, but it was locked. He walked around to the front window and saw Ramirez working in the back. Devin climbed through the customer service window, knocking over Isabella's workstation. Ramirez spotted Devin and ran to the other side of the pharmacy, pushing over shelves full of medication to block

Devin's path. Isabella saw the commotion and tried to restrain Devin, but he pushed her away. He continued to kick his way through the debris to get to Ramirez.

"DJ, stop!" Sparks yelled. People inside the pharmacy were screaming, unsure of what was happening. Sparks and Zach climbed through the window and managed to grab their friend before he could reach Ramirez. Devin was irate.

They took Devin back to the detachment, and he was immediately called into Chang's office.

"Look, I know you're hurt, but you cannot lose your composure. You've worked too hard to throw it all away. I just spoke to the Med Group Commander and explained the situation. He remembered you from a case briefing a few weeks ago, so he's willing to let it go. What I need from you is to go home, take a few days of leave, and when you're ready, we'll get back to it."

Devin felt like a shell of himself as he realized just how badly he had messed up. He turned in his weapon and walked out of the detachment.

Detective Kim was standing in the parking lot, smoking a cigarette. She walked over to Devin and grabbed his arm before he could enter his vehicle. "Look, I know you're going through a dark time right now. Some people step into the darkness and get overcome, but a true warrior fights his way out of the shadows."

Devin paused, trying to grasp what Detective Kim was trying to convey. Unable to fully understand, he drove away from the detachment. For the next few days, he chose to be alone, sulking in his apartment. He thought alcohol might help dull the pain, but he quickly realized it only made things worse. Sparks and Zach stopped by periodically to check on him, but he never opened the door. His cell phone constantly vibrated with messages, but he had no desire to check it, unaware of how deep his depression had become.

After a few days, Devin finally decided to leave his apartment and walked across the airbase. Just as the fresh air began to lift his spirits, he noticed a newspaper on the ground with Ella's face on the cover page. Anger welled up inside him, and he continued walking until he found himself back at his apartment, consumed by his own regrets.

At the detachment, work continued as usual, with Zach and Sparks conducted several interviews each day. As they wrapped up their tasks, they wondered how long it would take for Devin to return to his normal self.

"Look, man, I feel sorry for the guy, but I don't know what to do. I tried calling, texting—he doesn't want to talk," Zach said.

"Yeah, same here," Sparks responded. "I stopped by his place a couple of times, but he won't come to the door. To be honest, if he did open the door, I'm not sure I'd know what to say."

As they were speaking, Detective Kim arrived and walked over to her desk. "Do either of you know how to reach his family? Maybe they can help him," she said.

Sparks shook his head. "Nah, I don't know anyone … well … maybe."

That evening, Devin sat alone in the corner of the bar at the NCO Club, slouching on the bar stool. Tori, who hadn't spoken to Devin in several weeks, walked to the bar entrance and stopped when she saw him. She took a moment to compose herself before approaching him. When she felt ready, she walked over and placed her hand on his back. Devin saw her approach in the reflection of the glass behind the bar.

"Devin, I'm sorry that you're hurting," she said softly.

Devin turned toward her, acknowledging her presence. He cast his eyes downward almost immediately, but not before she saw his eyes were bloodshot.

"I didn't know Ella personally, but if she was someone you cared about, then she must have been a wonderful person."

Without looking up and in a voice barely loud enough for her to hear, Devin asked Tori how she knew where to find him.

"Sparks called my office and asked me to check on you." She assumed the bartender must have given Sparks a heads up that Devin was not looking too good.

"Tori, I appreciate your concern, but I just need a little time to get my mind right. I'll be alright," Devin said, taking another swallow of his drink.

"I know you will," Tori replied, "but I want you to know that you don't have to rush, and you don't have to be alone."

Devin turned to Tori with a look of confusion but couldn't bring himself to meet her eyes. "I just keep asking myself, why did I take her out that night? If I had just let things be, none of this would have happened."

Relieved that Devin was opening up a bit, Tori replied, "D, it's not fair to blame yourself. You didn't hurt her. All you did was give her a reason to smile. And although all of this is so sad, she was lucky to have you by her side when she needed someone."

Seeing the physical toll the grief was taking on him, she offered to buy Devin another round and asked what he was drinking.

"It was just a Coke," Devin answered.

They both laughed, and Tori suggested they go for a walk. Devin agreed and suggested a familiar location.

Tori and Devin left the NCO club and walked about half a mile across the airbase. Devin led her to the back of the gymnasium, where they sat together on top of a hill, watching the fighter jets take off and land on the runway. Talking about the commotion on the flight line seemed to distract him from his grief. Over the next few days, Tori made it a point to spend time with Devin, helping him get out of his apartment—first with bowling, then basketball. She wasn't trying to replace Ella; she was just trying to replace the sadness.

When Devin seemed to be getting back to his old self, he and Tori decided to grab a burger from one of the fast-food restaurants on base. Tori decided to ask the question that had been on her mind for the past two years. "Why didn't you call me?"

With a mouth full of French fries, Devin replied, "What do you mean? I called you this morning."

Tori chuckled, realizing that Devin's quick response without fully understanding the question was a good sign he was feeling better. "Nah, D, that's not what I meant. Why didn't you call me after you left Hickam?"

Sensing the conversation was about to take a serious turn, Devin took a big sip of his soda, buying himself a few seconds to find the right words. "I don't know. Why didn't you call me?" He knew it was a cowardly response, but that's all he had at the moment. Tori responded, "I didn't call you because I thought you probably hated me for what happened before you left. I didn't exactly handle things the best way, and I know you expected and deserved better from your girlfriend."

Devin wasn't comfortable with the conversation, but he was honestly surprised it had taken this long to get to it. "To tell you the truth, I didn't know what to think. I mean, you made it very clear that you didn't want to follow where I was going and that if I wanted to keep you in my life, I had to choose between you or a future without you."

Reflecting on that night, Tori found it hard to maintain eye contact with Devin. "It seemed to me that your mind was already made up before you told me, and I was upset because I felt like I didn't really have a say in your decision. But now I see that it was your decision to make."

Devin leaned back in his chair, tapping on the table, trying to break the tension. "I kinda understand why you'd think that, but when I told you, I had just found out a couple of hours earlier.

I've replayed that conversation in my head a thousand times, trying to figure out where it went off the rails, and just so you know, if you had asked me to stay, I would have."

Tori was stunned and struggled to find her words. She knew that Devin wasn't ready to delve deeper into the conversation, and she didn't want to push him. Finally, she was able to look him in the eyes. "Well, neither of us can change the past, right?" She quickly changed the subject to the new menu items at the restaurant. Though it was an abrupt end to the conversation, Devin was relieved she didn't pursue it further.

CHAPTER 9
ASSERTION

After a few days of monitoring video feeds, Agent Chang received vital information from the Wing Commander and called a meeting in the conference room to share the news. That same morning, Devin returned to work. He walked into the office and paused at Ella's desk, staring at her picture, which remained untouched since she last sat there. Agent Chang noticed and approached him.

"Devin, are you good to go?"

Feeling more like his normal self, Devin replied, "Yes, as long as we can turn up the heat."

Chang nodded, and the two walked into the conference room to join the rest of the team. Standing at the front of the table with a confident smile, Chang began. "Ladies and gentlemen, I just got off the phone with General Lane. He's been pushing the State Department to do something about the trafficking issue in Songtan. The embassy has provided no guidance, so he's putting his career on the line and placing his trust in us. It's game time. We've been given the green light from the Pyeongtaek Magistrate and the Wing Commander, who believes this operation needs to happen now! Here's the plan: Detective Kim and the KNP team will lead the raids. We can't risk any issue with you guys being involved in Korean arrests. Once they've secured the locations, you'll go in and assist with rescuing the victims."

As Chang was speaking, Mullins stood to the side, appearing to have a secret she could no longer keep. "As you all know, the new assignments were released yesterday, but with everything going on, I wanted to wait until things calmed down before giving you the news. But I think now is the best time. I don't know how you did it, but all three of you are going to the Anti-terrorism Specialty Team, the AST. And judging from the work you've done here, the AST will be lucky to have you."

Mullins began passing out the documents to the agents, announcing their next assignments. "Sparks, McGuire Air Force Base, New Jersey, TALCE mission. Congrats." Sparks thanked Mullins, and for the first time in a while, he genuinely showed a sense of gladness, realizing he would be closer to his family in New York. Mullins then handed a document to Agent Zachary and announced that he was heading overseas to the UK. Finally, Mullins turned to Devin and quietly told him about his next duty station. "Devin, Hurlburt Field, Florida, Headquarters–Air Force Special Operations Command." The agents congratulated each other, excited about what would come after their tour in Osan.

Around 1300 hours that afternoon, the agents met with the KNP to finalize the plans, and then they struck. The KNP loaded up on several transport vehicles and began raiding the establishments in full SWAT gear. The bars were mostly empty at the time, but the owners were shocked at what was transpiring. The raids happened so quickly that even the bar owners, who had nothing to do with the trafficking, filled the streets and alleys to see what the commotion was about.

The OSI agents stood on the rooftops while the KNP cleared the locations. Once the agents received the 'all clear' from the KNP, they made their way down the fire escapes and entered the buildings. Turning on all the lights, they saw just how terrible the conditions were for the girls. Armed with bolt cutters, the agents began cutting the locks on the cages. Sparks and Zach provided aid to the victims, helping them out of the buildings. Devin searched the area and found drawers full of documents, including the girls' passports, photographs of their families, and other belongings.

As the agents secured the final location, they exited the building to find multiple Korean news cameras in their faces. The streets were full of people trying to figure out what was going on. Local hospitals had provided multiple ambulances to supply medical aid to the victims, some of whom needed to be immediately transported to medical centers for care. Only feet away from the ambulances, KNP wagons were filled with Korean bar owners being hauled away to the Pyeongtaek jail.

While the agents were conducting the operation, Agent Mullins was called to the Seoul Trauma Center as Capt. Brunell had regained consciousness. Mullins walked up to the desk, and the nurse pointed her toward Brunelle's room. When she entered, she found Brunelle sitting up, looking out the window. He had a patch over his right eye and several tubes running from his arms. As she approached, she pulled her credentials from her pocket to introduce herself.

"Captain Brunelle, my name is Special Agent Mullins with OSI. I heard you were awake, and I wanted to stop by and see how you were doing."

"I figured you'd show up sooner or later," Brunelle replied. "I wish it would have been sooner."

Agent Mullins slowly walked over to Brunelle's bed. "What do you mean?"

His uncovered eye was bloodshot, and his face was severely swollen. "They did this to me. They said it would all be okay if I just kept my mouth shut. I mean, the money was good, so I just turned my head," Brunelle whispered, struggled to comprehend why this had happened to him.

"Captain Brunelle, I don't know what you're talking about. What happened? Who did this?" Mullins asked.

"They were stealing medication and selling it off base—Oxy and Viagra. I caught them changing the numbers on the inventory. They said if I didn't report them, they would cut me in on the money. They thought I snitched to your agents, so they did this to me."

"Who did it?" Mullins asked.

Brunelle revealed the names of his attackers. "Staff Sergeant Ramirez and Tech Sergeant Wilson."

Back in Songtan, the agents and Detective Kim were wrapping up the raid operations. As the agents were downloading their gear, they looked up and saw Detective Kim approaching with a huge smile.

"I wanted to thank you guys for following up and getting this done. We made a dramatic difference today," Kim said.

Before leaving, they all decided to stay and help keep the victims calm until the medical personnel could treat them. While waiting beside the ambulances, Agent Sparks's cell phone began to ring. He saw Mullins's name on the caller ID and answered, expecting to provide an update on their operations. But he was surprised by the news and eagerly shared it with the rest of the team, putting his phone on speaker.

The agents gathered around as Mullins spoke to her team. "I'm at the trauma hospital in Seoul. Brunelle just woke up and confessed to helping steal opioids from the pharmacy and selling them to the bar owners. He also named who tried to kill him."

"Who?" Zach asked.

"Wilson and Ramirez," Mullins answered.

Devin and Sparks looked at each other, stunned by how deeply they were involved in the situation.

"I just got off the phone with JAG. You've got verbal approval for an arrest on Wilson and Ramirez. Go get 'em."

Sparks hung up the phone as the team tried to come to grips with the new developments. Realizing that Devin and Sparks may have triggered the attack on Brunelle, Zach was eager to take action. "We need a plan, fellas."

Sparks checked his watch and surveyed the scene. "It's almost 1600. I guarantee you they're in one of these clubs."

Devin nodded. "Then let's hit them all until we find them."

The three agents parted ways with Detective Kim and began going from bar to bar, searching for Wilson and Ramirez. They stopped Town Patrol and asked if they had seen either of them. Although they hadn't, they agreed to join the agents in their search.

The agents arrived at a crowded pub halfway down a side street, a location none of them had previously visited. As they entered the establishment, they separated and began slowly walking through the crowd, scanning the area for Wilson or Ramirez. While moving through the sea of people, Devin caught a glimpse of someone who looked like Wilson but couldn't positively identify him due to the many people blocking his view.

In the middle of the crowd, Wilson caught sight of Sparks walking through the pub, appearing to be searching for someone. Realizing it was time to leave, Wilson began to swiftly move along the wall toward the exit. Devin spotted him and tried to push his way through the crowd, but the throng of people made it difficult. Frustrated, Devin pulled his badge from under his shirt and shouted, "I got him! Police! Move out of the way! OSI! Move!"

Zach noticed the commotion and began making his way to assist in the arrest. Wilson, seeing Devin clear the crowd, decided to rush him before he could react. He tackled Devin to the ground, and the two became locked in a struggle. Devin managed to kick Wilson off him, but Wilson quickly grabbed a bottle and smashed it on a nearby table.

The crowd began to panic, with people trying to force their way out of the escalating situation. Devin stopped in his tracks as he saw Wilson holding the jagged glass. Realizing he was in over his head, Wilson grabbed a girl from the crowd and held the broken glass to her neck, using her as a shield to edge toward the exit. "Get out the way! Move! I'll slice this bitch! Move!"

Wilson inched closer to the door, desperately searching for a way out of his predicament. Just when he thought he could slip out of the club and disappear into the alleys, Sparks blindsided him, tackling him to the ground. Town Patrol stormed the club with their weapons drawn, alerted by the fleeing crowd. They quickly placed Wilson in handcuffs and escorted him out of the club. The main route back to the airbase was lined with people watching the commotion. Town Patrol led Wilson through the district in custody, with the agents following close behind.

Standing among the crowd was Tori; she had been out shopping with her friends when she noticed the gathering around the pub. She had no idea what had happened but suddenly spotted Sparks, whose hands were bleeding from broken glass. She looked a little further and saw Devin; his forehead was bleeding, and his shirt was torn. The crowd murmured about what might have occurred as they watched Wilson being marched in front of them in handcuffs. Clearly concerned, Tori called out to Devin, "D! DJ! you good?"

Devin looked over, saw the worry on Tori's face, and continued walking. "I'm about to be."

As Wilson continued his humiliating march in handcuffs, he looked to his left and spotted Ramirez standing at the back of the crowd, smoking a cigarette and pretending to talk on his cell phone. Their eyes locked, and Ramirez seemed to revel in the fact that Wilson would no longer be in his way. With a menacing smirk, Ramirez turned his back and walked away.

Town Patrol took Wilson back to Osan and escorted him to the OSI detachment. Once he was secured in the interview room, the agents returned to the bullpen and watched him over the monitor for about forty-five minutes. Agent Mullins arrived back from Seoul, eager to start the interrogation. "Alright, who's up?" she asked.

Sensing Devin's need for redemption, Zach handed the lead to him. "DJ, it's all you, man!"

As Devin and Sparks made their way to the interview room, Sparks grabbed Devin's arm. "Hey man, damn the rapport. Get in his ass!"

Sparks sat at a desk in the corner of the room, while Devin pulled up a chair and positioned it directly in front of Wilson, who immediately seemed uncomfortable with Devin's invasion of his personal space.

Wilson expected the agents to start with small talk, thinking he could chat his way out of any serious trouble. He was wrong. Devin reached into his pocket and pulled out his rights advisement card. "I am Special Agent Devin Jackson, a member of the Air Force Office of Special Investigations." The weight of the moment crashed down on Wilson, and he became terrified by the seriousness of the agents' demeanor.

As the interrogation ensued, Wilson tried to resist, offering multiple explanations for what happened to Captain Brunelle. Each time he denied involvement, Devin would move his chair closer and call out his lies. Wilson cycled through a litany of emotions, from screaming his innocence to banging on the table and making threats. But none of it worked. Devin kept pressing, interrupting Wilson every time he spoke. Although Wilson was extremely flustered, he didn't confess to the attempted murder.

Devin paused his questioning and looked over at Sparks, who handed him a cell phone. Devin played a video of Brunelle's confession to the drug theft and naming Wilson and Ramirez in the assault. Wilson became emotional, realizing he couldn't escape the consequences of his actions. Two hours into the interrogation, Devin was still hammering Wilson with questions. Finally, Wilson gave up, lowered his head, and confessed "yes" to all the violations the agents had accused him of.

As the interrogation wound down, Sparks finished reviewing his notes with Wilson. Satisfied they had everything they needed, Devin and Sparks stood to leave the room. Devin opened the door and was about to exit when Wilson interrupted him.

"Hey, Jackson, there's one more thing. I knew Ramirez was going to hurt Brunelle, but I didn't tell him to kill your girlfriend."

Devin and Sparks froze.

"What did you say?" Sparks asked.

"I was tired of y'all messing up my money, so I told him to put something in Jackson's drink, just enough to make him sick. His dumb ass put it in the wrong drink, and he put too much. I didn't know that was gonna happen."

Before Devin could react, Sparks yanked Wilson from his chair and slammed him against the wall. Agent Zachary rushed into the room and pulled Sparks into the hallway.

Devin sat at Ella's desk, seemingly in a trance, as Sparks and Zach tried to figure out how to handle Wilson's statement. Although Devin managed to keep his composure, he knew he wouldn't be calm enough to finish the interview, so he asked Sparks to take over. After a few minutes, Sparks and Zach resumed questioning Wilson.

"Where's Ramirez now?" Sparks asked.

"I don't know," Wilson responded. "I haven't seen him in two days. He's on leave until next week."

Devin listened to the conversation through the monitor, still seated at Ella's desk, staring at her picture. Sparks, uncertain whether to trust Wilson's accusation, questioned his motive for turning on his partner.

"Why are you snitching on him?" Sparks pressed.

"Because he cut me out. We were supposed to be selling the dope to the Koreans and splitting the money. He went behind my back and started selling directly to the Ukrainians, then the Koreans blamed me for cutting them out."

"Ukrainians?" Sparks asked, surprised.

"Yeah, he started taking trips down to Busan. I thought he had a girlfriend there. Then more pills started disappearing, and I couldn't cover it on the inventory. He's got to have a connect down there somewhere."

Sparks walked out of the interrogation and signaled for the Town Patrol to come in and take Wilson to the holding facility on base.

Without saying a word, the agents began packing their body armor and extra magazines, then separated into two vehicles. They were united in their mindset: justice was coming to Ramirez that night. Detective Kim arrived and joined the team as they exited Osan, heading south on the peninsula to the city of Busan. Devin drove the first vehicle accompanied by Sparks, while Zach and Detective Kim followed in the second car.

The ride was quiet, each of them processing the moment introspectively. During the drive, Sparks pulled out his cell phone and made a call to Agent Yang at the Busan detachment. The conversation was brief, but Sparks seemed to get the information he was seeking. After nearly three hours of traveling, the agents reached the city. It was just after midnight, and the streets were bustling as usual. The skyline was lit with a multitude of neon lights, so bright they illuminated the inside of the vehicles.

Sparks received a text message from Agent Yang: "All good. Standby for address." As soon as the address came through, Sparks pulled out a second phone and sent a message.

Around this time, Kovalenko and his team were meeting at a construction site inside an unfinished building in downtown Busan. Ramirez, after abandoning his former boss Wilson, had officially earned Kovalenko's trust and was about to take a seat at his table among the other members of the crew. Kovalenko waved Ramirez into the room.

"So, Staff Sergeant Ramirez, as you can see, when you're willing to do the hard things, you can be rewarded. I didn't think you would leave Wilson behind, but you saw the big picture, didn't you? By the way, where is he?"

Not wanting to jeopardize his chances of joining Kovalenko's crew by revealing Wilson's arrest, Ramirez nervously took his seat. "I don't know where he is. I think he saw the writing on the wall and knew he needed to get out of the way."

"So be it," Kovalenko said as he began to address his team. "Gentlemen, let's get started. This will be my last meeting here with you. I'm being pulled back to the States to fill another void in our business. The family will send my replacement … Wait, where is my daughter? I need her here now. Somebody get her on the phone and find out where she is!"

On the other side of town, Devin arrived at the Intercontinental Hotel and dropped Sparks off at the front entrance. Sparks walked inside and took a seat at the hotel bar. Devin waited in the parking lot across the street, while Zach positioned himself half a mile down the road. Inside the hotel, Sparks kept checking his phone while pretending to babysit his drink. He heard footsteps and looked up to see Sophia approaching him.

"Al, I'm surprised to hear from you so soon. Is everything okay?" Sophia asked as she sat down at the table.

"Yeah, everything's fine. I found myself back in town for the night and wanted to see you."

"Ah, okay. Well, I have to work tonight, but I have a few minutes, I guess," Sophia said, glancing around nervously to see if any hotel staff might recognize her.

Sensing her unease, Sparks decided to test her story. "Oh, I'm sorry. I didn't see you at the front desk when I checked in, so I assumed you had the night off."

Sophia laughed and responded, "Oh, yeah, I have the night off from here, but I'm working at my other job tonight." As she spoke, she received a text message and quickly put her phone back in her purse.

"Well, since you're here now, how about joining me for a drink?" Sparks suggested, motioning for the bartender to come over.

Still looking uncomfortable, Sophia searched for an excuse to leave. "Yeah, Al, I don't really think I can tonight." She received another text message. "Tonight's just not a good night for me. Can I please take a rain check?"

Sparks knew better than to push too hard, so he gave her an out. "Well, that's disappointing, but yeah, I understand. Gotta pay the bills, right? Just text me if you have some time later."

Sophia quickly stood up and grabbed her purse. "Sure, Al. Thanks!" She began to walk away but paused and turned back to the table. "Are you sure everything is okay?"

"Yeah, it's fine," Sparks replied, lifting his glass as she turned to leave.

As Sophia exited the hotel, Devin, positioned across the street, spotted her immediately. Speaking into his body-worn radio, Devin alerted the team. "I've got eyes on her. She's leaving now, heading north in a red two-door Nissan, right toward you."

Agent Zachary acknowledged the transmission. As Sophia pulled out of the hotel parking lot and began driving down the highway, she passed by Zach's location. He smoothly merged into traffic to follow her. Meanwhile, Sparks, who had just left the hotel, jumped into Devin's car, and they trailed behind Zach, maintaining a cautious distance.

Detective Kim called out Sophia's directions over the radio as Zach maintained a loose vehicular surveillance. Sophia navigated her car slowly through the heavy traffic, which allowed Zach to keep several cars' distance between them, preserving his cover. Finally, Sophia made a right turn onto a side road.

"She's making a right turn, DJ. Pick her up," Kim said.

Devin took the lead on the surveillance, parking his car on the side of the road to monitor Sophia's movements. Zach circled the block and parked at the opposite end of the street. The agents observed as Sophia walked through a construction area and entered what appeared to be an unfinished office building.

Once Sophia was inside, Zach moved his car closer to Devin's, and the agents convened to discuss their game plan. As the senior agent, Zach gathered everyone to ensure clarity on their objective. "Alright, listen up. We're not here for the Ukrainians. We're here for Ramirez. We'll deal with the Ukrainian situation later. Everybody got it?"

"Yep, as long as they don't get in the way," Devin replied with a smirk, popping the trunk of his car. The agents began donning their body armor and black OSI raid jackets. They split up again—Devin and Sparks entered the building through the same entrance as Sophia, while Zach and Detective Kim circled the exterior, searching for a separate entry point.

Inside the building, in what appeared to be a future conference room, several armed men loyal to Kovalenko surrounded a large rectangular table. His daughter, Sophia, stood among them. Listening to the loud conversations emanating from the conference room, Devin and Sparks climbed four flights of stairs and located Sophia's position. The conference room walls were fully covered in drywall, but the adjacent room was only framed, providing an ideal vantage point for the agents.

Ramirez, now a fully integrated member of Kovalenko's team, stood at the end of the table and emptied a large bag of pills. "Guys, I believe this is what you were looking for."

"Nice work, Ramirez. I'm always impressed by how bright your future could be," Kovalenko responded as he inspected the pills.

Most of Kovalenko's men were uneasy about Ramirez's presence among them. "Boss, I don't get why this American is here," one of them complained.

Before Kovalenko could respond, Ramirez interjected. "Like I told your boss, you can get it cheaper from me than from those Korean dudes. I never liked dealing with them anyway."

"Yes, but why are YOU here?" the man pressed.

"What do you mean?" Ramirez asked, playing innocent.

The man walked over and stood directly in front of Ramirez. "Where is Wilson?" he demanded, making his distrust clear to everyone in the room. Sensing her father's growing irritation, Sophia stepped in to defuse the situation.

"I tried calling Wilson several times, but he never answered," she said.

Ramirez knew that if the Ukrainians discovered OSI had arrested Wilson, they might kill him to keep him from talking. His best bet was to continue feigning ignorance. But the Ukrainian mobster remained suspicious. He turned to Sophia. "Call him now!"

Sophia reached over to the table and pulled her phone out of her purse. After unlocking it, she navigated to her recent calls. Her last call had been to Wilson, but as she attempted to redial, she accidentally tapped on the second number on the list—Sparks's number.

In the next room, Devin and Sparks were leaning against the frame and drywall when Sparks's phone suddenly began to vibrate. "What is that noise?" The angry mobster, alerted by the sound, started scanning the room for its source.

By the third vibration, everyone was on edge, trying to pinpoint the cause of the noise. The angry man walked around the table, convinced he had located the source. "It's coming from behind the wall!" he shouted.

Without hesitation, he drew his pistol and fired several rounds into the wall, just a few feet away from where Devin and Sparks were concealed. The two agents quickly scrambled for cover behind the nearby construction equipment.

Zach and Detective Kim heard the gunfire and immediately dashed up the makeshift fire escape. As the Ukrainians picked up on the noise Devin and Sparks made while scrambling for cover, they fired several more shots into the wall.

The angry Ukrainian man turned to Ramirez, his suspicions now seemingly confirmed. "Did you set us up?" he demanded.

Ramirez, visibly panicking, stammered, "What? I don't know what's going on!"

By this time, Zach and Detective Kim had reached the entrance to the floor via the fire escape. Zach quickly called over the radio, "Devin, Sparks, are you okay?"

Devin replied, "We're pinned down behind the conference room. Fourth floor!"

Devin and Sparks struggled to return fire as bullets ricocheted around them. Desperate, they exchanged glances, searching for a way out of the situation. Just then, Zach kicked open the conference room door and began firing from the hallway. Devin seized the lull in incoming fire and unleashed a quick burst of rounds into the room, striking one of the Ukrainian men, who collapsed and dropped his gun. Another shot shattered the chandelier, sending it crashing onto the conference room table. Shards of glass sprayed across the room, slicing Kovalenko's right hand.

Ramirez spotted Devin through the holes in the wall and grabbed the fallen gun before bolting for the back door. Sparks noticed Ramirez's escape and alerted Devin.

While the Ukrainians concentrated on firing at Zach through the main entrance, Devin and Sparks slipped out the rear door in pursuit of Ramirez. Meanwhile, Zach and Detective Kim continued firing into the conference room until one of Zach's rounds hit Sophia in the head, killing her instantly. Her body slumped onto the table before sliding to the floor. Before Zach could process what had happened, Sparks's urgent voice crackled over the radio.

"Zach, fall back! Fall back! We got Ramirez. He's heading to the street!"

Zach and Detective Kim immediately retreated to the fire escape as the Ukrainians gathered around Sophia, desperately trying to provide medical aid. "Who the hell was that?" the angry man demanded as Kovalenko sat on the floor, cradling his dead daughter in his arms.

After exiting the building, Devin and Sparks carefully searched the dark construction site for Ramirez. The area was littered with debris, providing ample hiding spots. As he lay low, Ramirez spotted Sparks approaching and began to aim his gun at Sparks. In the darkness, Sparks was unaware that Ramirez was less than ten feet away. As Sparks moved forward, he came more into Ramirez's line of sight. Ramirez began to squeeze the trigger when a loud BANG! echoed through the site—Devin had fired a round at Ramirez but missed. Realizing he was exposed, Ramirez immediately took cover and then bolted from the area.

Panicked and desperate to escape, Ramirez dashed wildly through the traffic in Busan, with Devin and Sparks close on his heels. The two agents, in far better physical condition, were relentless in their pursuit. Ramirez, gasping for breath, had to stop periodically to catch his breath, while the agents seemed to only gain strength as the chase continued.

Ramirez weaved in and out of traffic, narrowly avoiding several collisions. Devin and Sparks split up, each taking a different route to cut him off. Ramirez began to realize he couldn't outrun them much longer. Sparks cut through a parking lot and ended up running directly toward Ramirez, closing the gap. Devin was closing in from the rear.

Ramirez, now running on the sidewalk, spotted a bench between him and Sparks. He charged toward it, intending to leap over Sparks. With all his might, he leaped onto the bench with one leg and tried to vault over Sparks, but it didn't work. Sparks caught Ramirez mid-air and spun him around. At that moment, Devin used the same bench as a springboard, launching himself into Ramirez, knocking him over a turnstile and down a flight of stairs leading to the subway.

On the platform below, both Ramirez and Devin quickly got to their feet, bloodied from the fall. Ramirez stood under a light, while Devin remained in the shadows a few feet away. Ramirez glanced up the stairway and saw his gun lying on the steps where it had landed during the fall.

Ramirez, now unarmed, turned to Devin and began to taunt him. "Alright, man, you got me, you got me ... but do you really got me though?"

Sparks stood at the top of the stairs, his weapon trained on Ramirez. "You see what the deal is. Put your hands up!"

Feigning compliance, Ramirez slowly raised his hands. "My hands are up! Be cool!" He then turned to Devin. "Is this really what you want? You had to have your boy come save you? Huh? Is this how you want it? Too bad he wasn't there to save your pretty-ass girlfriend!"

Devin tasted blood on his lips and spat it onto the ground. His rage was palpable as he paced back and forth in the shadows, his eyes locked on Ramirez like a predator about to strike. Ramirez, ever the provocateur, continued to spit venom. "Well, since you're here, I might as well confess. I did it, but I wasn't trying to kill *her*. I was trying to kill *you*. That stupid bitch just drank from the wrong glass. That should have been you crying on the floor. That should have been you screaming like a little bitch … but I guess one bitch is as good as the next, right?"

Ramirez raised his hands above his head, blood pouring down the side of his face from the gash he sustained during the fall. "Is this what you want?" he taunted, grinning through the pain.

Devin glanced at Sparks, who still had his weapon trained on Ramirez. Sparks looked around for any witnesses before slowly lowering his gun. "Okay, do what you gotta do."

Seeing the gun lowered, Ramirez dropped his hands and faced Devin, who remained mostly hidden in the shadows. Ramirez wiped the blood from his eye and squared up, ready to fight. Suddenly, a kick struck Ramirez in the right leg, causing him to lose balance and stumble forward. Devin followed up with a flurry of punches and kicks to Ramirez's midsection, driving him back against the wall. Ramirez, regaining his composure, reached into his back pocket, pulled out a blade, and charged into the shadows where Devin waited.

Still standing in the stairwell, Sparks strained to see what was happening as most of the fight took place in the shadows. With the blade in his right hand, Ramirez swung wildly, slicing Devin's left bicep. Devin immediately jumped back, realizing Ramirez had a weapon. Emboldened, Ramirez attempted another strike. Devin dodged the initial swipe and quickly blocked Ramirez's arm as he tried to slice back across his body. Sliding closer, Devin put all his weight on Ramirez's arm, forcing it downward and causing him to lose strength in his grip. Sparks watched as the blade clattered across the concrete, coming to rest against the stairs.

Within seconds, the fight was over. Devin's silhouette loomed over Ramirez, who lay motionless at the bottom of the stairs.

Devin slowly emerged from the darkness, walking up the stairs just as Zach and Detective Kim arrived at the scene.

"Where's Ramirez?" asked Detective Kim.

Devin answered her without breaking stride. "Down there, bleeding."

Zach turned to Sparks, bewildered. "Bro, what happened here?"

Sparks chuckled. "Dude, that was the coolest shit I've ever seen in my life. Ramirez ran his mouth and got dealt with."

Detective Kim observed Devin's calm demeanor and marveled at how far he had come in the weeks since Ella's death. "Some people step into the darkness and get consumed," she murmured. "A true warrior fights his way out of the shadows."

Within a couple of minutes, the KNP arrived on the scene and coordinated with Detective Kim to take Ramirez into custody. The agents briefed the KNP about the construction site before heading back to their vehicles to download their gear and begin the long drive back to the airbase. By the time the KNP reached the construction site, Kovalenko and his men had disappeared, taking Sophia's body with them.

The agents arrived back at Osan just as the sun was rising. The streets on the base were beginning to buzz with activity as most of the population prepared to leave for work. The team pulled into the detachment parking lot and slowly began unloading their equipment from the cars.

As Tori jogged by the detachment, preparing for her upcoming physical fitness exam, she noticed the agents unloading their body armor. Realizing they had been working all night—she had seen them arrest Wilson about twelve hours earlier—she saw the exhaustion etched on their faces. Glancing at the other joggers passing by, Tori reflected on how most people would never understand the heavy burden these agents carried.

Inside the detachment, the agents were eager to wrap up and head home. Feeling the need to apologize for the events of the past few weeks, addressed the team. "Hey, fellas, just wanted to say I appreciate y'all having my back today."

Zach nodded and smiled. "It's nothing, bro."

Devin then turned to Sparks, who was removing his shoulder holster. "Al, man, my bad about the whole polygraph thing. I just wanted to believe there was a reason for everything, and I didn't know how else to prove it. But that wasn't the best way to handle it."

Sparks replied, "You're right, it wasn't, but it's all good. You handled yourself well out there, and my bad, dude—I didn't even see him pull the blade on you!"

Devin chuckled, thinking about what had happened. "Ha! It's nothing! To be honest, I didn't see it either until he sliced my arm."

Finally, after a grueling twenty-seven-hour shift, the agents left the detachment and headed home for some much-needed rest.

Down in Busan, Kovalenko sat alone in a dimly lit hotel room. A knock on the door was followed by the sound of someone swiping a room key to enter. A European woman, around thirty years old, walked in, carrying a manila folder. She placed it on the desk in front of Kovalenko.

"Father, I have Sophia's files," she said. "It seems she was trying to flip one of the OSI agents who showed up in Busan."

Kovalenko opened the folder and pulled out a photo of Sparks's passport. "Al Sparks," he muttered. "I don't care how long it takes—bring me the names of all those agents. No matter how long it takes. Do you understand?"

The woman smiled. "Yes, Father, it would be my pleasure."

Late in the afternoon the following day, the agents were back at work in the detachment, trying to catch up on paperwork after the recent excitement. Agent Chang and Agent Mullins strolled into the bullpen with a guest. Chang stood proudly before his team, thanking them for their hard work.

"Guys, can I have your attention for a moment? First, I want to pass on congratulations from the Wing Commander. You all did an outstanding job! Not only did you shut down a prescription drug ring but the work you did with the Korean National Police resulted in the closure of nine bars and, most importantly, the rescue of seventeen human trafficking victims. These victims are currently being examined and will be reunited with their families soon. And gents, there's one more thing. I'd like to introduce you to our newest administrative officer, Staff Sergeant Brianna Brock. Please join me in welcoming her to the team. And once again, congratulations on your new assignments."

Sparks and Zach quickly walked over to Brianna to introduce themselves.

"Hey, I'm Al. It's nice to meet you. Welcome to the team! If you need help with anything, I'm here," Sparks offered warmly.

"Thanks, Al!" Brianna replied with a smile. "It's nice to meet you as well."

Zach immediately extended his hand. "I'm Zach. Welcome to the detachment."

Still seated at his desk, Devin could feel Sparks and Zach eyeing him, uncertain of how he would react to Ella's replacement. Sensing their eyes on him, Devin stood and walked over to greet the young NCO. Before he could speak, Brianna addressed him first.

"So, this was Ella's desk? She was very pretty. I've heard wonderful things about her. She must have been an amazing person."

Surprised by her thoughtful words, Devin felt at ease. "Yeah, she was something special. She always made sure we were squared away. Even though we deal with some crazy stuff around here, she always knew how to make us smile."

Brianna flashed a big smile and extended her hand. "I'm sure you all miss her very much."

"Yeah, we do. I'm Devin, by the way. It's nice to meet you."

Devin shook her hand, then rejoined the other agents in the bullpen. As he settled back at his desk, he heard Brianna call Sparks over for help, prompting a faint smile from Devin as he focused on his work.

Two days later, the agents sat quietly at their desks, waiting for something to happen. The silence was broken when Brianna walked in. "Guys, he's here."

Ramirez was led into the interrogation room by Security Forces, who had taken custody of him from the KNP. After they removed his handcuffs, Ramirez sat alone, facing the camera mounted in the back corner of the room. Devin and Sparks entered the interview room, and as soon as Ramirez saw them, he slipped back into his cocky persona, reciting lyrics from a rap song.

Sparks took a seat at the desk in the corner while Devin pulled up a chair directly in front of Ramirez, who only grew louder with his disrespectful behavior.

"Are you done yet, Thug Life?" Sparks asked, calmly preparing the documents for the interview.

Ramirez smirked. "Yeah, let's go, you raggedy-ass 21 Jump Street-looking muthafuckas."

Devin leaned in closer, pulling out his rights advisement card, ready to begin.

"I am Special Agent Devin Jackson."

Ramirez looked away, refusing to give Devin the respect of meeting his gaze.

"A member of the Air Force Office of Special Investigations," Devin said.

Ramirez smirked and rolled his eyes.

"I am investigating the alleged offense of murder, of which you are suspected."

Ramirez's smile vanished as the gravity of the charges set in. "What did you say? Murder? Hey, yo, I ain't murder nobody. Yo, Sparks, get your boy, man! Yo, I ain't murder nobody!" Although Ramirez had confessed to Ella's murder during his fight with Devin, he assumed his words couldn't be used against him since only Devin had heard him. Confident he could deny the allegations in the interview and beat the charge, he put on a defiant front.

"I advise you, under the provisions of Article 31 UCMJ, you have the right to remain silent."

"Yo, fuck that shit! Let me out of here, man. I ain't got nothing to do with that. Look, if you knew what was good for you…you know what I'm saying?"

Wasting no time with small talk, Devin remained calm. "Why did you kill Staff Sergeant Ella Mae Stringer? We know all about your little opioid operation. But why did you have to kill her?"

Ramirez continued to put on a performance for the camera. "Opioids? What?"

Sparks placed a voice recorder on the table and pressed play. Captain Brunelle's voice was heard explaining the entire drug operation at the base pharmacy. "Wilson and Ramirez would cook the books every two weeks before our audit. When I found out about it, they said they'd cut me in on the money if I kept my mouth shut."

Ramirez became irate as he heard Brunelle's testimony against him, his anger shifting from Devin to his former accomplices.

Noticing Ramirez's surprise at the video evidence, Devin leaned in, his voice more animated as he pressed. "Why did you kill Ella?"

Emboldened, Ramirez finally met Devin's gaze. "I told your monkey ass, I didn't kill that yella bitch!"

Ramirez was convinced he could outsmart the agents, but his confidence wavered when Sparks played another recording—this time, Wilson's statement outlining Ramirez's involvement in Ella's death: "I was tired of y'all messing up my money. So, I told him to put something in your drink, just enough to make you sick. His dumb ass put it in the wrong drink, and he put too much. I didn't know that was gonna happen."

Silence engulfed the room as Ramirez sat, the gravity of his situation dawning on him. The realization of the horror he was facing was beginning to display throughout his countenance. Panic began to creep into his expression. Devin continued the interrogation, each word pulling Ramirez deeper into memories of his evil acts that led him to that moment—the many times he sexually harassed Isabella in the pharmacy, the lives he ruined by selling opioids to service members. The intensity of the interrogation caused Ramirez to avert his eyes, unable to face the agents.

Devin sensed Ramirez's weakening resolve, slid his chair back, and retrieved a case file from the table. He opened it, revealing photos of Ella's casket. Ultimately, the sight became too much for Ramirez. He broke down, grabbing Devin's arm and pleading for help. But Devin didn't relent.

Ramirez began sobbing, whispering, "I'm sorry, I'm sorry." Within minutes, Ramirez fully confessed to Ella's murder, the attempted murder of Captain Brunelle, and his role in the stolen opioids.

Devin and Sparks exited the room, leaving Ramirez to draft his written confession. Back in the bullpen, the agents exchanged congratulatory nods and watched as Security Forces took Ramirez back into custody. Brianna, who had observed the entire interview from the video monitor, sat at her desk in astonishment. "Damn, this place is intense… I like it!"

The following three weeks saw a semblance of normalcy return to South Korea. With operations winding down, the agents were consumed by the humongous task of documenting their actions. Before they knew it, their twelve-month tour on the peninsula was nearly over. Since Devin had been the first to arrive, he would also be the first to leave Osan.

On the eve of his departure, Devin, Zach, Sparks, and Detective Kim gathered for one final dinner as a team. "So, what's up? Are you going to miss this place?" Detective Kim teased.

"Can't say that I will," Devin replied with a smirk.

Zach was equally unsentimental. "Well, tell you what, I'm not gonna miss Mullins screaming my name every five minutes."

Sparks laughed and nodded. "I heard that. Don't tell her I said this, but she did start to grow on me after a while."

The team shared a laugh together one last time before Detective Kim raised her glass for a toast. "To Ella," Zach said, raising his glass.

"To Ella," Sparks echoed.

Finally, Devin, feeling like he had been waiting for this moment for weeks, raised his glass. "To Ella Mae."

After dinner, Devin walked through the hallway of one of the dormitories on the airbase. He stopped at a door and knocked twice. Tori opened it, standing there with curlers in her hair. Embarrassed, she tried to cover her head.

"Hey, what's up, Curly?" Devin teased.

"Hey, Devin," Tori responded, attempting to hide behind the door.

" I wanted to see you before I head back to the States. Can I come in for a minute?" Devin asked, stifling a laugh at her awkwardness.

Tori opened the door wider, letting him in. "I heard you got a new assignment. Where are you headed next?

"The Florida panhandle. What about you? Your tour's almost up, right?"

"Six more weeks here, then I'm off to Andrews Air Force Base outside D.C.," Tori replied.

They stood there looking at each other for a moment, unsure of the status of their relationship. Sensing the need to keep the visit brief, Devin thanked Tori for helping him during a challenging time. "It's been a rough few weeks, and I really appreciate you having my back."

"Come on, man. I've got you. You know, sometimes I wonder what my life would be like if I hadn't walked away that night," she said, trying to gauge his response.

"Yeah, me too. Who knows…maybe one day we'll find out," Devin said with a faint smile.

Tori smiled back. "Yeah, maybe one day."

They embraced and said their goodbyes.

The next morning, Devin stood with his bags at the Osan bus stop, watching as the bus to Incheon International Airport approached. As it began loading, he took one final look around, remembering all that his team had accomplished and everything he had lost, then boarded the bus. The early morning hour allowed him to sleep for most of the two-hour ride.

At the airport, Devin passed smoothly through security and began boarding his flight. Walking down the aisle, he noticed a man ahead struggling to lift his bag into the overhead bin. "Here, let me help you with that," Devin said, easily pushing the bag into place.

"That's mighty kind of you, sir. You must be a service member," the man said.

"Yes, sir. Air Force," Devin said.

The man's interest piqued. "Really? What kind of work do you do?"

Without hesitation, Devin replied, "I'm a jet mechanic."

"Well, thank you for your service, and thanks again for the help," the man said, continuing to his seat.

Twelve hours and three questionable meals later, the plane touched down at Hartsfield-Jackson International Airport in Atlanta. Devin retrieved his luggage from baggage claim and wheeled his bags toward the exit. As he was walking away, Devin passed the man he had helped and overhead part of his phone conversation. "Yes, thank you very much. I'm always amazed at how bright the future can be," the man said.

The words stopped Devin in his tracks. They sounded eerily familiar. He recalled helping the man with his bags and remembered that his hand had been injured—just like the mob boss who had been injured during the shootout in Busan. The man on the plane was Viktor Kovalenko.

Without turning around, Devin's hand instinctively reached for his weapon, but it wasn't there. He had turned in his gun before leaving Osan. He stood frozen, watching Kovalenko's reflection on a flight monitor as he walked away.

Later, Devin rented a car at the airport and drove to Decatur. Three hours later, he found himself walking through freshly cut grass toward a large headstone beside a recently covered grave. The flowers from the funeral were still there, although a few had begun to wither, and some had been toppled by the weather. Devin struggled to hold back tears as he looked away, unable to bear the sight of Ella's name carved into the stone.

Finally, he found the courage to dare a glimpse at her grave before speaking. "Hey El. It's me. I'm sorry I couldn't make it to the funeral. I had some unfinished business to take care of." He paused, composing himself. "I spoke to your parents. They seem like really nice people. I wish I could have met them earlier. … The guys are doing good. You'd be proud of them. They'll be back stateside in a few weeks. I, uh, I wanted to say, I'm sorry. I promise, if I could trade places with you, I would … I miss you, El."

Devin knelt beside Ella's grave and placed a beautiful array of flowers next to her headstone. He then stood and placed an OSI coin on top of the marble. Taking one final look, he turned and walked away, unsure if he would ever have the courage to return.

A few days later, after receiving his personal belongings from storage, Devin drove down to the Florida panhandle, eager to see what his new assignment had in store. As he pulled up to the main gate at Hurlburt Field, his attention was drawn to the sign on the fence: "Air Force Special Operations Command—Any Time, Any Place." He had no idea just how much that slogan was about to change his life.

ABOUT THE AUTHOR

Derrick Jackson has been a jet mechanic, criminal investigator, counterintelligence agent, Certified Fraud Examiner, corporate investigator, and Inspector General.

He has traveled to over 30 countries conducting investigations, threat assessments, and intelligence activities. He served 21 years in the United States Air Force and retired as a Special Agent with the Air Force Office of Special Investigations (AFOSI).

Derrick lives in Virginia with his family and spends his free time with his sons. He enjoys watching college football (Roll Tide) and telling stories about ordinary people who accomplish extraordinary things.

www.ingramcontent.com/pod-product-compliance
Lightning Source LLC
Chambersburg PA
CBHW050506160726
48003CB00001B/192